Presented to:

_____

From:

_____

Date:

_____

365 Devotions to Love God and Love Others Well

Victoria York

365 Devotions to Love God and Love Others Well

Copyright © 2018 by Zondervan

Requests for information should be addressed to:

Zondervan, 3900 Sparks Dr., SE, Grand Rapids, MI 49546

ISBN 978-0-3100-8547-8

Cover design: Kathy Mitchell

Interior design: Lori Lynch

Printed in China

18 19 20 21 22 23 24 /DSC/ 12 11 10 9 8 7 6 5 4 3 2 1

Introduction

We all have something in common: everyone wants to love and be loved. We try to forge close relationships with our parents, our friends, or someone special, even our pets. It's part of the human DNA; it's who we are and how God designed us.

Our culture reflects this desire. Single people increasingly utilize multiple dating websites, while millions of weddings are performed every year worldwide. Social media sizzles with people desperately reaching out to each other, searching for perfect love.

But even amid fulfilling relationships built on the best intentions, inevitably, someone will fail us. This, too, is part of the complex human nature; but it's *not* who we are and *not* how God designed us.

Lean into the warm embrace of someone who loves you perfectly, who will never let you down, and who is always there for you. God knew you before you were formed (Jeremiah 1:5). He has a hopeful plan for your life (29:11). And He paid the ultimate price for you when He sent His Son to die on the cross for you (John 3:16). God not only adores you, He *is* love (1 John 4:8).

As you read this devotional, allow yourself to feel the powerful, never-ending love of God as it surrounds you. And as you experience the warmth that comes from growing closer to God, you'll discover that your own heart expands to love others even more.

JANUARY

....

The LORD loves righteousness and justice;
the earth is full of his unfailing love.

Psalm 33:5

Never-Ending Growth

Be joyful. Grow to maturity. Encourage each other. Live in harmony and peace. Then the God of love and peace will be with you.

2 Corinthians 13:11 NLT

The skeleton of a human being stops growing during young adulthood. We might put on the pounds, but we don't technically keep growing. However, quite a few plants and animals (called *indeterminate growers*) never stop growing. Sharks, coral, lizards, snakes, lobsters . . . even wallabies and kangaroos are on the list!

However, there *is* one way humans can continue to grow, and that's spiritually. If we strive each day to know and love the Lord a little more than we did the day before, we'll become more and more like Him. Spiritual growth never has to stop for the Christian because God is limitless, and so is His love. The universe, which never stops expanding, reflects this quality. We'll continue to grow closer and closer to God until we see Him face-to-face in glory. Can you imagine stepping more and more into the love of God until we are made complete in Christ?

I don't want to stagnate, Lord. Help me to keep growing in You, day by day. Amen.

Loved and Valued

For the LORD your God. . . . will take delight in you with gladness.
With his love, he will calm all your fears. He will rejoice over you.

Zephaniah 3:17 NLT

Maybe you've seen this object lesson: Someone pulls a crisp, clean twenty-dollar bill out of his billfold and asks if anyone wants it. Of course everyone says yes. Then the person crinkles up the bill, throws it on the floor, and stomps on it. He rubs some dirt on it and crumples it some more. Finally he asks, "*Now* who wants it?" Even though the bill looks as if it's been through the apocalypse, everyone still wants it because it hasn't lost one iota of its intrinsic value.

Because you're loved by your Creator, you are priceless beyond measure. Your intrinsic value doesn't change one bit regardless of what kind of day, week, or even year you're having. No matter how battered and beaten you feel. In spite of how many times you've been tempted to throw in the towel.

God has called you beloved and irreplaceable, and that settles that.

I choose to believe You when You say You delight in me, Lord. I
believe I'm more valuable to You than I could ever imagine. Amen.

Created with Love

Thank you for making me so wonderfully complex! Your workmanship is marvelous.

—Psalm 139:14 NLT

"Eeeewwww!" wailed the teenager as she looked at her senior photos, her mother and the photographer peering over her shoulder. "I look *awful!*" The girl's mother was frustrated, but the photographer was distressed. Those photos were a reflection of her skill. She'd put her heart into the lighting, setting, and all the other details. But the high schooler was so focused on herself and her flaws, she didn't realize her criticisms were also an attack on the photographer.

Do we do the same to our Creator? Do we focus only on our flaws? Instead of being thankful for strong legs to carry us across our favorite hiking trails, we grumble about "cankles." We wallow in self-loathing, oblivious to the message behind our complaints: "God, I know You put Your heart into it, but You did a poor job when You created me."

You are wonderfully and marvelously made by a loving Creator. Thank Him for that.

Lord, forgive me when I fail to recognize the love that went into Your creation of me—my body, my mind, and my personality. Thank You! Amen.

Good Bones

We are hard pressed on every side, but not crushed; perplexed, but not in despair; persecuted, but not abandoned; struck down, but not destroyed.

—2 Corinthians 4:8–9

These days, the trendy thing to do is snag an old house for a rock-bottom price and restore it: rip up the ratty carpets to expose hardwood; put fresh paint on the walls; knock down a few walls. The key to a great restoration project is that the house must have good bones—a well-built foundation and basic structure that will allow it to withstand time, weather, and so on. Restoring a house with good bones underneath the cobwebs means it'll stand strong for many more years. Otherwise, it's just a well-camouflaged shanty.

When our lives are built on God's love, we have spiritually good bones. We might go through some severe storms, but the love of God ensures that we'll be standing in the end. Whether we're struggling with bad health, the loss of a job, or the ending of a relationship, love gives us the endurance, resilience, and strength to live victoriously.

Lord, give me good bones! Fill me with Your Spirit so that my life is built on Your eternal, indestructible love. Amen.

Open the Eyes of My Heart

Let the rivers clap their hands, let the mountains sing together for joy.
Psalm 98:8

$\mathcal{J}$n all of creation, God reveals Himself. It's not that He *is* everything, and vice versa—that's pantheism—but it's that He speaks through what He's made. And why wouldn't He? When an artist creates a painting, it reflects at least one aspect of who he or she is.

Regarding the Ephesians, Paul prayed to the Lord, "Open the eyes of their hearts, and let the light of Your truth flood in. . . . Reveal to them the glorious riches You are preparing as their inheritance" (1:18 THE VOICE). You can ask God to do the same for you. As He opens the eyes of your heart, you'll see, hear, and otherwise sense God's presence and love in ways that others miss, and you'll find great joy in them. The more He speaks to you through rain or music or sunlight, the more aware you'll become of His affection for you.

Jesus, I know You surround me. Help me see Your presence, every single day. Amen.

Loving Discernment

Accept the one whose faith is weak, without quarreling over disputable matters.

Romans 14:1

Anna and her friends love board games. They play Monopoly almost every time they get together. And Anna doesn't mess around. She'll snag Park Place or Illinois Avenue in a heartbeat. She's ruthless.

However, the last time she played Monopoly with her ten-year-old daughter and her buddies, Anna "accidentally on purpose" made several mistakes that ultimately cost her the game and allowed one of the children to win. Why? Because love knows when it's time to play hardball and when it's time to take it easy.

Many of us like bouncing theological ideas off each other. If we engage in a friendly debate with a seasoned believer who can handle the difficult stuff, fine. But when it comes to someone who's spiritually younger, we have to be discerning. A discussion about doctrine that would strengthen a strong believer might damage a weaker one. There's no reason to be condescending, but gentleness is priceless.

Lord God, give me sensitivity and good judgment, and help me hold my tongue when I'm tempted to say too much. Amen.

The Gift of Feedback

Anxiety weighs down the heart, but a kind word cheers it up.

Proverbs 12:25

Have you ever received feedback that you deeply appreciated from someone? Maybe you asked a friend to look at your résumé, and he showed you how to tweak it to make it stand out from the crowd. Perhaps a boss commented on the way you helped streamline the workflow in your department. Every human being has a deep need for feedback. Without it, we have no idea where we stand. We aren't sure if we're doing a great job or just a mediocre one.

Love takes the time to give feedback. Think about the people you spend your days with. How do they add to your family, church community, or workplace? Be specific. Instead of "Your sermon was great," say, "Your description of the twenty-four elders made heaven come alive for me!" And if someone specifically asks for feedback, feel free to give both kudos and constructive criticism, as long as you end on a positive note.

Lord, please show me someone who could use some feedback, and then give me the words to encourage and build up that person. Amen.

Honest Speech

*Those who guard their mouths and their tongues keep themselves
from calamity.*

Proverbs 21:23

Try this experiment: Say the phrase "You did a good job" four
times, but each time—just by using a different inflection or
tone of voice—try to convey one of these distinct meanings:

"You did a good job . . . even though I didn't expect it."
"You did a terrible job."
"You did a substandard job at best."
"You did an amazing job!"

Were you able to do it? Most of us can easily imply at least
three of the four meanings because tone of voice is so powerful.
Have you ever been guilty of saying one thing while meaning
something altogether different? Our loved ones pick up on
those subtle rises and dips in tone, inflection, and volume.
They absorb the messages behind our words. When our literal
words don't match our tone, loving communication breaks
down and feelings get hurt. Ask the Lord to teach you to be
more lovingly authentic and sincere with your words.

*Lord, I want to communicate with both kindness and complete
honesty. Help my heart to match my words so that I speak in love at
all times. Amen.*

Tokens of Love

Therefore we do not lose heart.

2 Corinthians 4:16

Abby had been suffering from depression and desperately needed some small token of God's love for her. One January day, she decided to go for a run—a discipline she'd neglected for weeks. As she crested a hill, she noticed a row of young trees. Each one boasted tiny pink blooms. At this time of year, that was impossible—yet there they were. Rather than chalk it up to a fluke of nature, Abby saw it as a wink from God, that token of His love she'd been looking for. And for the first time in many weeks, she felt a spark of hope.

January is often a cold, dreary season. If you feel that way in spirit as well, ask God for a token of His unceasing love for you—but don't overlook it! Sometimes He speaks in unmistakable ways, but sometimes He's more subtle. Always be on the lookout for His small gifts.

Sometimes my soul is heavier than usual, Lord. When that happens, please send me a token of hope, and help me to recognize it. Amen.

You Look Like Your Father

Those who look to him are radiant; their faces are never covered with shame.

Psalm 34:5

One day, you meet a young woman for the first time, but you're convinced you know her from somewhere. After a few minutes, you connect the dots and realize that her father is an old friend you haven't seen for years. You're struck by how much she resembles your friend. "Wow," you say. "I feel like I'm talking to your dad!"

Later, you realize that as you looked at this young woman, you were also looking at your old friend. That's because his life was inside her, and vice versa. She was part of him, and it showed. So it is with Jesus and those who belong to Him. When you spend time with Him, His love will shine through your eyes. People will look at you and see the One who's inside you.

Do you want to be one of the radiant ones? Then spend time with Jesus, love Him, and look to Him.

I want to look just like You, Father God. In fact, I want people to look at me, but see You. Amen.

Love Incarnate

Humans only care about the external appearance, but the Eternal considers the inner character.

1 Samuel 16:7 THE VOICE

People are often drawn to the followers of Jesus without knowing exactly why. It's an attraction that has nothing to do with the literal, physical beauty our society is so obsessed with. Rather, it's a beauty that comes from within, and no one exemplified this truth better than Jesus. In fact, Isaiah tells us that Jesus "didn't look like anything or anyone of consequence—he had no physical beauty to attract our attention" (Isaiah 53:2 THE VOICE).

In the past, moviemakers portrayed Jesus as a pale, frail man. In more recent years, they've chosen handsome actors to play the part. But it's likely that neither representation is accurate. The Savior's appeal wasn't based on "beauty or majesty." Instead, His whole being hinged on love—love of the Father and His people. He was love incarnate. That drew people to Him. And that same selfless love will draw them to you.

You are my beautiful One, Lord. Teach me to look to You daily, until I radiate with Your light. Amen.

Be Slow to Judge

"[God] causes his sun to rise on the evil and the good, and sends rain on the righteous and the unrighteous."

Matthew 5:45

John's auto detailing business was doing great. He had so many customers he could barely keep up. Person One commented, "Wow, God is really blessing John!" Person Two, who wasn't as fond of John, answered, "Don't be so sure about that. I've always heard that if the devil leaves you alone, you're not doing something right!" Six months later, when John's business tanked, Person One assumed it was an attack from the devil, while Person Two insisted there must be sin in John's life.

We've all been guilty of looking at the circumstances of a person's life and then judging the genuineness of his or her faith. But loving one's brothers and sisters means resisting the temptation to judge on appearance. Christians go through suffering *and* happy times—but so do atheists, borderline believers, and everyone in between! When life throws someone a curveball, remember that love assumes the best. Be slow to judge and quick to help.

Open my eyes to the suffering of my Christian brothers and sisters, Lord, and then prompt me to lend a hand however I can. Amen.

The Art of Listening

Listen, open your ears, harness your desire to speak, and don't get worked up.

James 1:19 THE VOICE

Have you ever been talking to someone, laying your heart out there, when you realized he was barely listening? His body language revealed he was feeling fidgety and impatient. All he wanted was for you to stop talking so he could offer his own two cents' worth.

Too often, when we should be listening, we're actually busy forming our response. We've already moved on. We might be able to parrot what the person has said because we've heard it on a superficial level, but we've given no thought at all to what she's feeling or to the deeper meaning behind her words. And she knows it.

If you want to love others well, learn how to truly listen. Don't hijack the discussion so that it becomes about you and your own experiences. Engage the other person by asking questions. Cultivate compassion and patience. The art of listening is rare, but well worth learning.

I want to love others by listening with patience and empathy. Help me, Lord, to give my full attention to those who need it. Amen.

Room to Grow

Rebuke the wise and they will love you.

Proverbs 9:8

Karen's teenage daughter was livid. Her basketball coach had chided her in front of the other players. "She says I'm not a team player!"

Karen's first instinct was to side with her daughter, but then she remembered what she'd learned at Bible study: *Love does not always rescue.* Karen had a hunch that the coach was not just being mean. "Why do you think Coach might have said that?" she ventured. "Is there a chance she's onto something?"

We're all tempted at times to quickly defend those we care about, but love allows others to own their mistakes. The next time you suspect your child, friend, spouse, or colleague is facing a tough lesson, resist the temptation to make excuses for his or her behavior. Instead, ask questions and then wait for that person to formulate an answer. In the long run, that person will appreciate your honesty and willingness to give him or her room to grow.

Help me to step back, Lord, when I'm tempted to jump in and rescue someone who is facing an opportunity to grow. Amen.

A Big Deal

To one who listens, valid criticism is like a gold earring.

Proverbs 25:12 NLT

The *New York Times* ran a story in 2006 about a legal dispute between a Canadian cable TV provider and a telephone company. The ruling cost the cable company the American equivalent of $888,000. The clincher is that the ruling hinged on one tiny, misplaced comma within a fourteen-page document.[1] Sometimes the things that seem like no big deal are a very big deal.

This is also true in our interactions with the people we love. Sometimes we inadvertently step on someone's toes. When we realize that person is upset, we say, "You're making a big deal over nothing." But what seems like an inconsequential detail to you is a big deal to the other person for a valid reason. Maybe you unintentionally hit a nerve. Take a moment to consider all angles . . . and remember the comma.

I know that one of the most loving things I can do is to take people seriously when they say I've hurt them. Give me patience and compassion, Lord. Amen.

What Would They Say?

Follow my example, as I follow the example of Christ.

1 Corinthians 11:1

One of the most eye-opening exercises in self-evaluation is to ask yourself how those closest to you would answer certain questions. For example, what would your spouse say if someone asked, "Does _____ have integrity? Is he or she generous? Selfless?" What would your kids say if someone asked, "Is Mom/Dad honest? Patient?" What would your best friend say is most important to you?

Another thing to consider is whether or not you hope your kids, nieces, and nephews will one day follow in your footsteps and emulate your behavior. Do you hope they imitate the way you treat other people? How about your work ethic?

Paul was able to say, "Follow my example, as I follow the example of Christ." We might think this was an arrogant statement, but if we're truly loving as Jesus does, why wouldn't we want others to imitate us?

Lord, let it be said of me that the people in my life would do well to follow me as I follow You. Amen.

Creative Motivation

Let us consider how we may spur one another on toward love and good deeds.

Hebrews 10:24

ove is creative. One way to increase harmony and decrease stress in your household, workplace, school, or church community is to find ways to motivate others creatively—without threats, whining, or other immature tactics. For example, the next time you want a reluctant colleague to do his part of a tedious task, resist the temptation to say, "Stop fooling around on Facebook and help me." Instead, mention his aptitude with numbers: "I could really use your expertise with these financials. Can you give me a hand?" See if he isn't quickly motivated to help you when he realizes you appreciate his strengths.

Often, we take the easy way out by speaking impulsively ("You haven't asked me out to lunch in ages!"). It takes effort and creativity to inspire people in new ways ("I love your company. How about we catch up over lunch on Tuesday?"). But we'll quickly discover it's well worth the effort.

Thank You, Lord, for the people who add to my life. Help me love them well and motivate them in creative ways. Amen.

Love Shields

Gossip separates the best of friends.

Proverbs 16:28 NLT

When something is repeated again and again, even truth can become contaminated until it no longer resembles the truth at all. We've all been victims of gossip, and we've all contributed to the mess at least once. But love protects. It shields people from slander and unnecessary drama.

Ask yourself: *Are people's reputations safe in my hands? What do I normally do with knowledge I have about others that I find intriguing? Do I immediately get on the phone to share the news with someone else, or to analyze and dissect a situation?*

How can we know when it's okay to share a piece of news versus when we should keep quiet? When in doubt, we should treat what we know as confidential. If we don't have specific permission to share something, our duty is to consider it private. Make sure the reputations of other people are always safe with you.

Forgive me, Lord, for the times I've participated in slander and added to the drama of a situation. Teach me to love by knowing when to be silent. Amen.

Reconnecting

Brothers and sisters, my joy and crown whom I dearly love, I cannot wait to see you again.

Philippians 4:1 THE VOICE

𝓘 can easier teach twenty what were good to be done, than be one of the twenty to follow mine own teaching," wrote William Shakespeare in *The Merchant of Venice*. Can you relate to the poet's words? Do you find it's easier to know *what* to do than to actually do it? We all have good intentions, but do we see our plans through to the end?

Sometimes love in action is as simple as entering an appointment into your calendar. Have you ever reconnected with an old friend, realized the friendship was too valuable to neglect, and promised to get together again soon . . . only to fail to follow through? The mistake was failing to simply choose a date—you knew what to do but didn't do it.

Is there someone with whom you need to reconnect? Before another minute passes, pick up the phone or send an e-mail, and settle on a day and time.

Speak to me, Lord, and tell me who I need to reconnect with. I commit to put love into motion and follow through with a plan. Amen.

Flying Blind

"I will ask the Father, and he will give you another advocate to help you and be with you forever—the Spirit of truth."

John 14:16–17

𝓘n the 1920s, airplane instruments could convey details such as altitude, speed, and direction, but a pilot couldn't land a plane unless he could see his surroundings. By the end of the decade, however, it was finally possible for a pilot to both fly and land in conditions where visibility was difficult or even impossible, such as fog. In 1929, Lieutenant James Doolittle made a successful fifteen-minute flight and landing without ever seeing the ground, thanks to improved navigation instruments.

When Jesus returned to the Father, He loved us so much that He gave us the gift of the Holy Spirit. And though we can't literally see Him, He is eager to guide us through every detail of life. Because of the Holy Spirit, we can fly blind—that is, we can live well, love well, hit our mark day after day, and successfully navigate through life even when circumstances get foggy and we can't see what's ahead.

Lord, You love me enough to make sure I'm never alone. Thank You for Your Spirit, who keeps me on course every day of my life. Amen.

Divine Encounters

As Jesus started on his way, a man ran up to him. . . . Jesus looked at him and loved him.

Mark 10:17, 21

Scripture describes a conversation between Jesus and a certain young man that was very brief, yet so important it became part of the book of Mark. Within seconds, Jesus was filled with love for the man. We might assume this was because Jesus is all-loving and, therefore, He has to love everyone. But what if there's more to the story? Have you ever felt an instant connection with a stranger? Perhaps you meet the friend of a friend at a birthday barbecue and within minutes you feel you've known him your whole life. Or the new client at the nonprofit where you volunteer tugs so hard on your heartstrings that you're almost in tears as you talk with her. Don't dismiss those feelings as insignificant. God might be allowing your paths to cross for a reason. Some of the briefest moments are the most meaningful in His eyes.

Help me to recognize and act on those moments when You're bringing someone into my life for a specific reason, Lord. Amen.

Keep Your Eye on the Prize

I press on to reach the end of the race and receive the heavenly prize for which God, through Christ Jesus, is calling us.

Philippians 3:14 NLT

Continuing education instructors and workplace training leaders will tell you that even adults will go above and beyond for the promise of a prize, no matter how small or silly. People who organize fund-raisers know this too—attendance is always better when an art show, 5K, or festival involves prizes. People love to know they're winners.

In Philippians, Paul compared this life to a footrace. The good news is that the love of God will save you and ensure that you're part of the race. And the better news? There's a prize waiting for you at the end, even if you don't do life perfectly (and rest assured, you *won't* do it perfectly). The best news of all is that heavenly prize isn't just heaven; it's Jesus Himself.

In this event called life, the starting line *and* finish line are established in the love of God, and receiving the prize means setting your sights on Him.

I want to do the best I can in this race, Lord. You're the Prize that makes those steep hills worth it all. Amen.

Hungry and Satisfied

All that I am aches and yearns for You, like a dry land thirsting for rain.

Psalm 143:6 THE VOICE

We all know what it's like to be so hungry we feel positively faint and then eat to the point of regret. Maybe we've worked all day in the yard, mowing grass and trimming bushes and working up a voracious appetite. Finally, an extra-large pizza arrives, and the first few pieces are heavenly. But after a while, we've had enough; then we've had too much, and then we don't even want to *think* about pizza!

Hunger for God is quite different. As we pursue Him, we find Him, and we're "satisfied as with the richest of foods" (Psalm 63:5), but we're never overstuffed. In fact, the hungrier we are for God, the more He satisfies us—and then we, in turn, feel an even deeper hunger, which He also satisfies. The result is a wonderful cycle of hunger and contentment. Our appetite for God becomes insatiable, and this is exactly as it should be.

Lord, You're the only One who can satisfy me, yet I want to hunger for You more and more. Amen.

Heart and Soul

"Do all that you have in mind," his armor-bearer said. "Go ahead; I am with you heart and soul."

1 Samuel 14:7

One day, Jonathan, the son of Saul, was itching to pick a fight with an army of idol-worshiping heathens. "Come, let's go over to the outpost of those uncircumcised men. Perhaps the LORD will act in our behalf," he said to his armor-bearer (1 Samuel 14:6). Though they were absurdly outnumbered, the armor-bearer had Jonathan's back. "Go ahead; I am with you heart and soul," he said (v. 7). Was the armor-bearer crazy? Reckless? Or ridiculously obedient? No, he was filled with faith and fiercely loyal. His job was to shore up and assist Jonathan, and he took it seriously.

Often, a person's greatest ministry is to be someone's armor-bearer. If this is your assignment, be assured you'll have moments when you're tempted to panic. But remember, this isn't about blind submission to a mere human being; it's about God's perfect will. When you trust God to protect and guide your "Jonathan," you can say, "I'm with you heart and soul."

Show me, Lord, if You've appointed me to be someone's armor-bearer, and then make me worthy of the calling. Amen.

Investing in the Next Generation

Mordecai had a cousin named Hadassah, whom he had brought up because she had neither father nor mother.

Esther 2:7

At one time, multiple generations did life together. They lived together under one roof, or on the same piece of ground, for many years. The result was that children were taught and influenced by their grandparents and other relatives. These days, the nuclear family is more isolated, much smaller, and often fragmented.

Nevertheless, there are still people who willingly invest in the lives of the next generation by loving and nurturing children who aren't technically their own. Was your life impacted by such a person? Was this individual a teacher, grandparent, uncle, aunt, spiritual leader, or family friend? In what ways did this person help guide you through life?

Consider calling or writing to express your thanks to these important people. Let them know their influence was meaningful. Describe the effect it had on you. Explain the ways they taught you about responsibility, or love, or true strength. And then follow their example and invest yourself in a young life.

Thank You, Lord, for the people who taught me the values and principles I needed. Bless them for their willingness to love and invest in me. Amen.

"Don't Go Away from Here"

Boaz said to Ruth, "My daughter, listen to me. Don't go and glean in another field and don't go away from here. Stay here with the women who work for me."

Ruth 2:8

R uth was the new girl in town. She was vulnerable, and gleaning was sometimes a risky job. So Boaz asked her to stay in his fields, in the company of his female harvesters. He did this for her safety.

What if Ruth had thought, *What a control freak! Who is he to tell me where I can and can't go?* She would have missed out on what God had planned for her—and His plans were very good!

God's love draws boundaries; it protects. It doesn't cheat us out of fun; instead, it spares us the grief, depression, and other suffering that inevitably follow on the heels of sin. Not that Christ followers don't experience suffering—because we certainly do! But when we go off on our own to indulge in certain behaviors after God has said, "Don't go away from here," suffering isn't just a possibility; it's inescapable. Trust God's love . . . and His boundaries.

I know that sometimes I challenge the boundary lines You've drawn in my life, Lord, and for that I'm sorry. Amen.

Loving the Churches

Who is weak, and I do not feel weak? Who is led into sin, and I do not inwardly burn?

2 Corinthians 11:29

Take time to read 2 Corinthians 11:23–29. In this brief passage, Paul said he'd been in prison, endured flogging and stoning, been near death "again and again," and received thirty-nine lashes five separate times. He'd been "beaten with rods" and lost at sea. He'd run for his life from robbers, Jews, Gentiles, and "false believers"; and he'd faced danger in the city and country and while crossing treacherous rivers. He'd also experienced exhaustion, overwork, thirst, hunger, nakedness, and hypothermia.

Have you ever seen such a laundry list of ways to suffer?

But Paul wasn't quite finished. One more thing caused him distress: his "concern for all the churches" (v. 28). His love and compassion for his fellow believers was so intense that even as he plunged across raging rivers, fled from enemies, and fought the waves of the open sea, his heart was with the churches. Ask God to help your heart beat with that same kind of love.

Lord, I want to love my brothers and sisters with the depth of love that Paul had. Enlarge my heart! Amen.

Just as We Are

God demonstrates his own love for us in this: While we were still sinners, Christ died for us.

Romans 5:8

"Jesus loves us as we are, not as we should be—because none of us are as we should be," said Brennan Manning, who authored many books about the deep love of God, even as he struggled with alcoholism.[2]

Manning didn't mean that Jesus is flippant about sin. What he did mean is that Jesus isn't waiting around for you to get your act together before He starts loving you. Instead, He loves you in this instant, with all your imperfections, flaws, and hang-ups.

If you're striving to be a better person or to develop in Christian character, good for you! Never stop moving forward! The Lord is cheering you on as you overcome the temptation to gossip with your girlfriends or fill your mind with impure thoughts or give in to addiction. But He's not withholding His love until you conquer every sin. You're radically, extravagantly loved—right this very moment.

I'm amazed by the love that You feel for me at this moment, Jesus. I receive it with open arms. Amen.

The Truth About Denominations

We, too—the many—are different parts that form one body in the Anointed One. . . . We become together what we could not be alone.

Romans 12:5 THE VOICE

In some American cities, there's a church on nearly every street. Christianity now includes so many denominations (roughly three hundred just in the United States) that few of us have even heard of all of them.

Since church splits are a sad reality, many people assume those three hundred denominations resulted from arguments within the church. While some *did* come about because of disagreements, most were motivated by passion for God. Because someone wanted to carry the gospel of Jesus to a new group or in a new way. Or because someone longed to live a life he believed was closer to God's perfect will. The vast majority of denominations within Christianity were created because of *love for God* rather than *hate for one's brother in Christ.*

In spite of doctrinal differences, your church and the one down the street most likely have the one thing in common that outweighs everything else: they are rooted in the love of God.

Bring harmony to Your church, Lord! Help us remember that we're united by what's most important—the love of You. Amen.

Melting Ice

Gracious words are a honeycomb, sweet to the soul and healing to the bones.

Proverbs 16:24

You're running late. You grab your car keys, dash out the door, and attempt to hop into the car, only to discover that the doors are frozen shut. And the deicer is in the trunk—which is frozen shut too.

The next time this happens, make your own deicer from plain water and alcohol. Isn't it strange that these simple ingredients, both of which are usually right under our noses, create a solution that will instantly cut through ice?

In the same way, sometimes the simplest things will cut right through an icy situation. That new church member who always looks as if she's been sucking on lemons would melt in a moment if you invited her to lunch. The neighborhood boy who's always misbehaving would follow you to the moon and back if you took the time to bake him some cookies.

Hearts all around you are ready to be melted. Grab your deicer.

Lord, I know there are ways to love others that are simple but powerful. Teach me to apply them. Amen.

Love and Allegiance

One of you says, "I follow Paul"; another, "I follow Apollos";
another, "I follow Cephas"; still another, "I follow Christ."
Is Christ divided?

1 Corinthians 1:12–13

Picture a football field filled with people. A balloon is suspended dead center, high above the field. Now imagine a string stretching from each person up to that balloon. Even though countless people are standing all over the field, all the strings converge at the balloon. At that one point, every single person is represented and comes together with every other person.

In today's passage, the Corinthians were feeling smug, competing with one another in an effort to appear superior. They sounded like we sometimes sound today: "My church (pastor/denomination/Christian author/TV evangelist) is better than yours. Don't you know *my* way is God's way?"

Paul was frustrated because he knew that allegiance to a person versus God Himself never breeds love—only division. His message was always this: Look only to Jesus. Give your love and allegiance only to Him. Jesus is the point at which all Christians should converge because we share a common love for Him.

I pray for the church today, Lord. May every member ultimately look
to You and not to a person. Amen.

FEBRUARY

··

*"But to you who are listening I say: Love your
enemies, do good to those who hate you."*

Luke 6:27

Love and Perspective

The prudent hold their tongues.

Proverbs 10:19

"Are you going to eat that?"

"Try to be home a little early tonight, okay?"

"What did you do yesterday?"

The same question that sends one person into a tizzy can communicate love to the next person, and be completely neutral to the next. How? Perspective.

One of the keys to loving communication is the willingness to see things from another person's perspective. When you talk to someone, everything you say is processed through his or her frame of reference. That frame of reference consists of a person's experiences, beliefs, culture, educational background, emotional state, gender, age, and so on. Someone might be very close to your age and have similar beliefs and cultural background, but his or her frame of reference could still be very different from yours. Always remember this when you ask a question and get a response that's completely opposite of what you were expecting. Back up, rephrase your question, and lovingly try again.

Lord, when someone hears what I say in a skewed way, may I be loving, patient, and forgiving. Amen.

Love Is the Greater Good

Live in true devotion to one another. . . . Be first to honor others by putting them first.

Romans 12:10 THE VOICE

You return from a weeklong trip to find that your mom, who housesat during your absence, has rearranged every plant, candle, and end table in your house so that everything flows better. What do you do? What do you say?

Some things are priceless and, therefore, worth protecting, even when that means making a sacrifice. And what's more priceless than love?

How do you protect the love you have for friends and family, as well as their love for you? By surrendering your right to be right. Some issues must be hashed out, but many others aren't worth discussing, much less fighting about. So your mother went a little crazy with your décor. You can spend ten minutes moving everything back, or you can start a quarrel. In this case and many, many others, sacrificing your right to speak your mind could deflect a lot of hurt feelings. Are you willing to hold your tongue for the greater good of love?

Dear Father, I want to protect the love I feel for my family members and friends. Help me to be quick to sacrifice my right to be right. Amen.

Your Desires, God's Desires

Take delight in the LORD, and he will give you the desires of your heart.

Psalm 37:4

He'd always said he'd rather walk on broken glass than do public speaking. But here he was, looking forward to leading his next seminar.

The thought of managing a roomful of kids had always made her panic. But now she couldn't stop thinking about volunteering for the Sunday school position.

Have you ever felt compelled to do something you normally wouldn't do? Or realized you wanted something you never wanted before? Psalm 37:4 doesn't mean that first you want something, and then God buckles and gives it to you. It means that first *He wants something for you*, and then He sets things into motion so that your desires line up with His will.

The things we want aren't always what we need. But the things God wants for us will bring us more joy and fulfillment than we ever imagined. When loving God is our first objective, we'll end up loving what He loves . . . and He'll give us the desires of our hearts.

Please, Lord, change my heart and my mind so that my desires line up perfectly with Your will. Amen.

Ask for Help

God is our refuge and strength, an ever-present help in trouble.

Psalm 46:1

A young man loses his brother in an accident. To cope with the grief, he turns to alcohol. A year later he's a full-blown alcoholic. Looking back, he says, "I should've asked for help."

How many of us have gone through unnecessary suffering because we refused to ask for help?

Sometimes people experience something so traumatic that they carry the aftereffects with them for a very long time—maybe even a lifetime. If this sounds like you, it's time to ask for help. You can and should ask someone you trust, but you absolutely *must* ask the Lord, as well, if you want to be permanently free. He loves you so much that He suffered and died to liberate you from that thing that haunts you. Invite Him to help you. He *will* come, and He'll carry your burden for you. Let the love of God free you from the pain and shame. Ask for help.

Lord, I humble myself and ask for help with this thing that troubles me. I can't free myself, but I know You can. Amen.

Sledgehammer or Flyswatter?

A rebuke goes deeper into a man of understanding than a hundred blows into a fool.

Proverbs 17:10 ESV

When you were a child, were you easily corrected? Did you settle down as soon as your mom gave you "the look"? Or did you need more convincing? When some kids misbehave, a single word will put them back on track, while others require a firmer hand. Loving parents recognize what each child requires.

If you're in a position of authority and part of your responsibility is to instruct and correct others, you've probably discovered that adults are the same way. Some will change their behavior with the slightest reproof, while others aren't as pliable. The key is to remember this rule of thumb: "Don't use a sledgehammer when a flyswatter will do the job." In other words, if criticism is needed, use wisdom and care. Take the person's personality into consideration. Is a formal write-up necessary, or would a gentle admonition be more than enough? Love is tactful and as kind as possible while still being honest.

Help me to be mindful, Lord, of the personalities of every person I supervise. Teach me to give correction and instruction with love and kindness. Amen.

God's Loving Correction

Flog a mocker, and the simple will learn prudence; rebuke the discerning, and they will gain knowledge.

Proverbs 19:25

We—God's children—need constant correction from our heavenly Father. No matter how hard we try to get it right, we stumble and sin. Because He loves us beyond our understanding, God will do whatever it takes to get us back on track. He does so for our own good, to keep us from irreparable harm—but He's not malicious. He prefers to nudge gently, though we must be willing to respond to that gentle nudge.

If we're malleable and quick to obey, responding willingly to the Lord's voice when He corrects us, we'll avoid unnecessary grief and perhaps even disaster. We'll also have more time, energy, and opportunity to be about the Lord's business.

God loves all His children, even those who aren't so responsive to His correction, but imagine how much more fruitful our lives would be if we determined to be sensitive to His voice and respond quickly.

Forgive me for the times I've resisted You, Lord. I promise to try to respond promptly when You correct me. Amen.

Walking on Water

The boat was . . . buffeted by the waves because the wind was
against it.

Matthew 14:24

At eighteen, Amy still didn't have her driver's license. The idea of steering three thousand pounds of steel down the open road petrified her. But her father knew she was severely limiting her options by not having a license. So one day, as dad and daughter took a drive down a country road, he stopped the car and said, "We're stuck here till you take us home."

Amy was speechless. She was also anxious . . . and angry. But when they pulled into their own driveway an hour later, she was behind the wheel.

A wise person once said, "Because He loves us, the Lord will sometimes allow the storms so He can teach us to walk on water." Often, when we face a dilemma or struggle, we fret and whine, "Why me, Lord?" Meanwhile, He's saying, "Get out of the boat and do something you've never done before. I'm inviting you to grow, mature, and experience something new."

Lord, I'm thankful that You love me enough to send certain storms so
that I'll grow and learn to love You more. Amen.

Tight Spots

But Jonah ran away from the LORD and headed for Tarshish. . . .
Now the LORD provided a huge fish to swallow Jonah.

Jonah 1:3, 17

Just as God allows storms for our own benefit, He also allows us to get ourselves into tight spots, as Jonah did when he tried to run from God. Picture it this way: Your left foot is on one side of a crack in the sidewalk and your right foot on the other. Suddenly the crack starts to widen. For a while (especially if you're flexible), you can keep each foot in place, spreading your arms for balance. Finally, however, you realize you'd better make up your mind and shift your weight to either the right or left if you don't want to fall in.

God allows predicaments that feel a lot like this because He knows we're prone to paralysis (especially those of us who tend to overthink and second-guess every situation). God's love will cause a fissure beneath our feet so we'll get moving, make a change, and do whatever it takes to get on with the business of godly living.

I understand You sometimes allow me to get into predicaments to free me from inaction. Thank You for loving me enough to help me get unstuck! Amen.

The Small Stuff

Like clouds and wind without rain is one who boasts of gifts never given.

Proverbs 25:14

Have you ever heard someone say, "I'll give a million or two to charity if I ever win the lottery"? If the person is generous to begin with, you might believe her claim, but if she doesn't share what she already has, her good intentions don't carry any weight. Someone once said, "The smallest deed is better than the grandest intention." Promising to give away a million dollars someday is one thing, but making a difference right now is another.

Look around. You might be able to change someone's whole day through a small deed—for example, a bag of a favorite coffee for a friend who needs a pick-me-up, with a note that says, "Just because you're loved." Sometimes we just need to know someone's thinking of us.

While some folks are busy spouting off about doing the big stuff and then not following through, love makes a lasting impact by doing the small stuff.

I want to do the small stuff, Lord, because small things can make such a big difference. Show me how to bless someone today. Amen.

Walk Like a Man

He has told you, O man, what is good; and what does the LORD require of you but to do justice, and to love kindness, and to walk humbly with your God?

Micah 6:8 ESV

Clint Eastwood in *A Fistful of Dollars*. John Travolta in *Saturday Night Fever*. John Wayne in virtually every movie he ever made.

Each of these actors had a unique walk, a saunter, or a strut meant to communicate, "I'm strong and confident. I'm a force to be reckoned with. I'm a real man."

But what does it really mean to walk like a real man—or woman—of God? According to Micah 6:8, it means qualities such as a desire for justice (or, as some translations read, a desire to do what's right) and a love for kindness (or mercy). It also means humility—acknowledging one's total dependence on God. These are the qualities "the LORD require[s] of you."

There's nothing wrong with being a big, burly man—or a resilient, capable woman—whose literal walk reflects strength and confidence, as long as your spiritual walk reflects humility and love.

Lord, may I walk the way You desire a godly person to walk—in humility, kindness, and love. Amen.

When We Had Nothing to Give

"For God so loved the world that he gave his one and only Son, that whoever believes in him shall not perish but have eternal life."

John 3:16

The man cared for his son around the clock. It had been eleven years since the boy had suffered a brain injury—and since he'd recognized his own father. Still, the man exercised patience and compassion, even on the most difficult days.

"Don't you sometimes want to throw in the towel?" someone once asked him. "He doesn't even know you!"

The man looked baffled by the question. "But I love him."

God loved us so much that He gave His most beloved gift even though we had nothing to give Him but our sin. He knew that many people would not only ignore Jesus but despise and revile Him. Yet He did it anyway.

It's been said that "the measure of a man is how he treats someone who can do him absolutely no good." To love as God loves means there are no strings attached. Will you love without expecting anything in return?

You loved me, Lord, even when I had nothing to give You. Even now, all I can give You is my love and obedience. Help me to do that well! Amen.

Who You Once Were

If anyone is in Christ, the new creation has come: The old has gone, the new is here!

2 Corinthians 5:17

Is there someone in your life whom you love dearly but whose life before knowing Jesus was filled with major mistakes? Has that been difficult for you to deal with?

When we love someone, we must understand that the experiences in their past—including every noble deed and every wretched sin—have shaped them into who they are today. Because God is a God of redemption, He uses our circumstances, and even our mistakes, to mold and break and change us. He is able to use the chaos and heartbreak that come from promiscuity and abortion to turn a girl into a woman with a heart for adoption. He can use a man's ten-year battle with alcoholism to turn him into an effective and empathetic counselor.

Love acknowledges who you once were. Love sees no reason to sugarcoat, deny, or be afraid of past mistakes. Love doesn't require an apology over and over again. Love understands we're a new creation.

Lord, help me to release all fear, jealousy, and anger in regard to the mistakes that _____ made in his/her past. Thank You for making all things new. Amen.

Who You Will Be

For those God foreknew he also predestined to be conformed to the image of his Son.

Romans 8:29

Imagine a scale from one to ten. "Ten" is the person who insists her loved ones can do no wrong. She downplays or explains away every flaw, no matter how serious. "One" is the person whose loved ones can do nothing right. He overlooks every good quality, choosing to nitpick and criticize instead.

When you love people in a healthy way, you sit at or near a "five." You clearly see not only who a person is at the moment, but also who she *will* be. You hold a crown a few inches above her head and encourage her to grow into it. You extend the grace he needs as an imperfect human being while also challenging him to be who God calls him to be.

If you desire to love others well, pray they'll be conformed to Jesus' image (versus your own image or some impossible standard). Recognize their potential, while making room for mistakes along the way.

Lord, teach me to give my friends and family grace when they fail while also gently challenging them to be more like You. Amen.

Valentines Day

Love Is the Goal

"And lead us not into temptation, but deliver us from the evil one."
Matthew 6:13

There's a comical YouTube video featuring three dogs competing in an obedience test. One by one, dog and trainer stand at opposite ends of a path strewn with squeaky toys, hot dogs, and such. The trainer gives the command—"Come!"— and the dog's job is to obey without getting distracted by all the goodies. Two of the dogs keep their eyes on their trainer and pass with flying colors. The third bolts straight for the first hot dog, then pounces on a toy, then a dog biscuit, and so on, all the way down the line.

We're all like that third dog sometimes. Love is the goal, but so many temptations vie for our attention: petty offenses, feelings of superiority, feelings of self-condemnation, spitefulness, unforgiveness, and jealousy. Loving well requires obedience and discipline. Thankfully, our great Trainer never gives up on us. Keep your eyes on Him and remember . . . love is the goal.

Lord, I do want to be a loving person and immune to distractions.
Give me strength! Amen.

Be Made Whole

When Jesus saw him lying there and knew that he had already been there a long time, he said to him, "Do you want to be healed?"

John 5:6 ESV

If you've ever taken a commercial flight, you've heard the spiel: *If the plane loses air pressure, make sure your air mask is secure before assisting the people around you.* We can understand why airlines offer these instructions: If we're floundering, choking, panicking, and inching toward death, we're no good to anyone else. But if we make sure we're out of immediate danger ourselves, we can then help someone else.

If you're floundering through life—tormented by unhealthy thoughts, trapped by addiction, caught in a deadly relationship, or otherwise stuck in a downward spiral—the best thing you can do for others is to say yes to the healing God has for you.

God has a wonderful plan for your life. There are people He wants you to touch and influence for good. But first, He wants to restore you through His amazing and healing love. Invite Him into every corner of your life, and let Him make you whole.

I want to be the best me I can be so I can help other people to do the same. Heal me, Lord. Amen.

Childlike Love

I cling to you; your right hand upholds me.

Psalm 63:8

Think about a time when you were little, and you snuggled in with your mom as she read you a bedtime book. You enjoyed her affection for you and loved her with abandon. Or maybe you adored your daddy, climbing up onto his shoulders every time you went someplace together. You couldn't get enough of him.

We're so uninhibited and receptive to love when we're little—before we're old enough to have had our hearts broken. We soak up our parents' displays of affection. We don't cringe; we don't balk. The Lord wants us to be like children, and this is the reason why. Even though God is spirit, not flesh, we can snuggle up with Him as we spend time with Him. We can lean on Him and be receptive to His affection for us.

If you find that you sometimes feel awkward or inhibited in the Lord's presence, ask Him to give you a childlike love.

Father, I want to be spontaneous and abandoned in my love for You. Let me love You the way a little child does. Amen.

Loving Creator

For since the creation of the world God's invisible qualities—his eternal power and divine nature—have been clearly seen, being understood from what has been made, so that people are without excuse.

Romans 1:20

I once heard a story about Ronald Reagan that goes like this: when Reagan was president of the United States, so the story goes, he once hosted a state dinner for the leaders of Soviet Russia. As everyone finished the superb meal, one of the Russians asked who the White House chef was. Mr. Reagan shook his head. "There is no chef," he replied. Thinking Reagan had misunderstood, the Russian again asked, "This meal was excellent. Who is your chef?" Again Reagan replied, "We have no chef. The meal came together all by itself." With this, the Russian got angry. "Sir, we are not planning to steal your chef from you. What is his name?"

The president looked kindly at the Russian. "Look, sir," he said. "You can believe that the whole universe came together by itself, but you can't believe a simple meal did?"

All we really need in order to believe there is a God—who loves us very much—is to look at the wonders of nature. Our Creator put the answer right in front of our eyes.

Everywhere I look I see evidence of the reality of You. Thank You for loaning us such a beautiful world! Amen.

The Spirit Who Loves

The Spirit gives us desires that are the opposite of what the sinful nature desires. These two forces are constantly fighting each other, so you are not free to carry out your good intentions.

Galatians 5:17 NLT

Have you ever had an internal argument with yourself while talking to someone who annoys you?

She's not so bad.

Are you kidding? I just want to scream right now!

C'mon, calm down. Give her some grace.

No! She doesn't deserve grace!

When a person is born again, his or her spirit is made new—but sometimes the emotions take a while to catch up. They aren't as easily cleaned up. If we allow our feelings to dictate how we respond to people, many of us would ostracize everyone who rubs us the wrong way. But we can determine to be controlled by the Holy Spirit rather than our emotions.

When a loved one says or does something that sets you spinning, realize it's your emotions that are reacting negatively, not your spirit. Your emotions want to lash out, while your spirit patiently loves and looks for the best in others at all times.

Lord, thank You for filling my spirit with Your Spirit. Help me live and love according to the Holy Spirit rather than my emotions. Amen.

God Answers

Jabez called out to the God of Israel: "If only You would bless me, extend my border, let Your hand be with me, and keep me from harm, so that I will not cause any pain." And God granted his request.

1 Chronicles 4:10 HCSB

One of the responsibilities of parenthood is to protect the child. No loving parent would grant a child's request if that request would hurt the child. Our heavenly Father, God, is the most loving and responsible parent there is, and He always knows what's best for us. Consequently, sometimes when we pray and make a request of Him, He'll answer with a definite no. Sometimes He loves us too much to say yes!

Read 1 Chronicles 4:10, commonly known as "the Prayer of Jabez," carefully. Notice the last phrase of Jabez's prayer: "so that I will not cause any pain." An earlier verse tells us that Jabez was a faithful and obedient servant to the Lord. So God knew Jabez's heart; He knew his motives for wanting extra blessings were pure and good. Therefore, He lovingly granted Jabez's request.

Model your heart—and your prayers—after Jabez, beginning today.

Thank You, loving Father, that Your answers to my prayers are always right. May my prayers always be in line with Your perfect will. Amen.

Love and Unity

[I] urge you to walk worthy of the calling you have received, with all humility and gentleness, with patience, accepting one another in love, diligently keeping the unity of the Spirit.

Ephesians 4:1–3 HCSB

If you've ever watched the Winter Olympics and sat spellbound as the four-man bobsled teams performed, you've seen teamwork so synchronized that it's almost like watching a professional ballet. Each member of the team has his specific job. And if any member is missing, wishing he had another member's position, or not fulfilling his responsibility, the whole team suffers and will undoubtedly lose the race. The job of the team just won't get done.

Churches must function in much the same way. Paul told us in Ephesians 4:1–3 that there must be teamwork, or the job of the church just doesn't get done. No one should covet another's job. Each person has his own calling and must perform his own job with diligence, humility, peacefulness, and gentleness, accepting every other member and his or her job with love. There must be loving unity for the church to fulfill its mission. And you must help keep that unity.

Lord, please help me find my role in the church and then fulfill it. May I always encourage love and unity in Your church. Amen.

Love Sees the Heart

Love never fails.

1 Corinthians 13:8

After sixty-eight years of marriage, George and Dorothy Doughty, ninety-one and ninety-two years old, died within hours of each other. They had never spent a day apart.[1]

The love that many elderly couples share is a mystery to the young. Perhaps that's because there are some things you just can't understand until you've spent a very long time loving the same person.

Couples whose marriages have stood the test of time will tell you that after fifty, sixty, or more years of marriage, a wife sees not a rickety, old man in overalls but a gallant, young man with strong hands, quick reflexes, and broad shoulders. He, in turn, sees the young lady with a sharp mind, pretty legs, and sparkling eyes that he fell in love with. Neither is blind to the truth. In fact, you could argue they see more clearly than anyone else.

Because love doesn't see age and wrinkles. Love sees the heart.

Lord, I want to see people's hearts, not the wear and tear on the outside. Give me clear vision. Amen.

More Than Conquerors

No, in all these things we are more than conquerors through him who loved us.

Romans 8:37 ESV

No one can deny that the conquest of Mount Everest in 1953 had to be one of the greatest accomplishments of humankind. After nine previous attempts by various teams, Sir Edmund Hillary of New Zealand and Tenzing Norgay, a Sherpa, were the first human beings to complete the 29,035-foot ascent.[2] Many people have died attempting this feat, and many have made no more than a partial ascent. The seemingly superhuman challenges of the feat have simply proved too much for most climbers.

Sometimes daily life presents us with apparently superhuman challenges. We might begin to feel a task is impossible. We might be convinced we've tried every possible route up the mountain of our problem, and now we stare up at the immense height of it and think, *I can't do this.* Well, maybe we can't. Not on our own. But with God—because of His immeasurable love for us—we are more than conquerors. We can do the impossible!

Lord, Your great love for me makes all things possible. When I face difficult problems, remind me that, through You, I'm more than a conqueror. Amen.

No More "Hey, You!"

Each of us should please our neighbors for their good, to build them up.
Romans 15:2

If someone offered you $500 to remember five random words for three hours, you'd have no trouble committing those words to memory, right? Yet why is it impossible to remember the names of five new people you meet at a party? Because in the first scenario, we had something to gain. What we fail to realize is that we also have plenty to gain by remembering a person's name.

We all love to hear our own names. We feel validated when someone says, "Hi, Kathy" versus, "Umm . . ." Calling a person by name is a way of honoring him or her, especially for those isolated from friends and family. That homeless man you see every day—have you ever called him by name? (Have you ever *asked* his name?)

"Love thy neighbor" refers not just to noble deeds, such as prison ministry and overseas missions, but also to the tiniest of gestures that communicate honor (Mark 12:31 ASV). Like remembering a name.

Lord, please remind me daily that sometimes the seemingly small acts can have the biggest impact on those I'm commissioned to love. Amen.

Divine Provision

The Jordan overflows its banks throughout the harvest season. But as soon as . . . their feet touched the water at its edge . . . the water flowing downstream stood still, rising up in a mass. . . . until the entire nation had finished crossing.

Joshua 3:15–17 HCSB

Four Utah police officers were trying to rescue a young woman from a car that was partially submerged, upside-down, in an icy river. They found the woman dead in the front seat. Thinking she was the only occupant, they began to leave when all four heard what sounded like another woman calling, "Help!" Returning to the car, they looked in the back seat, where they found a small child—still alive—strapped in a car seat. The child was rescued and survived.[3]

We often hear stories of miraculous rescues. Few, however, can compare with God's rescue of Joshua and the entire Hebrew nation as they came to the flooded Jordan River. There was no way for the people to cross, but, of course, nothing is impossible for God—He simply stopped the river from flowing. God loves His people so much, He provides a way through the impossible.

Thank You for loving me so much, Lord, that You'll even do the impossible to provide for my needs! Amen.

Gifts

For by grace you have been saved through faith. And this is not your own doing; it is the gift of God.

Ephesians 2:8 ESV

Everyone enjoys opening presents. Though sometimes we open them with a smidgen of trepidation because we know the contents are bound to be unwanted, considering who the gift is from. That pile of ties, fruitcakes, and ugly knickknacks in the closet just keeps growing!

There's one Loved One, however, whose gifts we would never relegate to a dark, forgotten corner: God. His gifts are always blessings. And unlike the people who send us gifts that *they* would like to receive, God grants us gifts that are just exactly what we need. His gift of salvation is the greatest of all these blessings, the incomparable gift. In Ephesians 2:8, Paul wrote that salvation "is not your own doing, it is the gift of God." In other words, we can never earn God's greatest gift. It is given—with no ulterior motives—because He loves us. We simply have to accept it.

Thank You, Lord, for the many blessings You shower upon me because You love me. Thank You especially for the gift of an eternity with You. Amen.

Consequences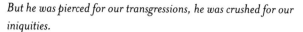

But he was pierced for our transgressions, he was crushed for our iniquities.

Isaiah 53:5

*I*f you've raised a teenager, you know that one of the most difficult principles a parent must teach is that everyone must suffer the consequences for his or her misdeeds. It's painful to watch your child struggle because of a wrong he's done, especially if it's something you could fix for him, but the value of the lesson he'll learn by writing a note of apology or serving detention at school is far greater than his consequential pain.

However, when Jesus died on the cross, He *became* all the sins humankind ever committed, all they were committing at the time, and all they would ever commit. He took upon Himself all the punishment, guilt, and shame those sins deserved. And He did that so that we who believe in Him won't have to bear the eternal consequences of our sins. There is no greater love than this.

Lord, You paid a very high price to free me of the eternal consequences of my sins. Thank You for Your inexpressible love. Amen.

Beautiful Boundaries

The boundary lines have fallen for me in pleasant places; surely I have a delightful inheritance.

Psalm 16:6

Few things will ruin a nice meal at a restaurant faster than a child whose parents let him yell and run around like a wild monkey. We shake our heads sadly because we know the child is going to suffer for being allowed to do whatever he wants. The overly permissive parents are asking for trouble, and their little one is bound to grow into a difficult adult.

Thankfully, God is the perfect Parent, who refuses to allow His children to do whatever they want or to get everything they ask for. Instead, He sets limitations on our behavior because He loves us. We might pout and fuss and even accuse Him of being unfair, but, as we continue to grow in Him, we'll eventually see that we've been spared a great deal of suffering thanks to His boundary lines. Because sometimes love means saying no.

Show me, Lord, if I'm rebelling against the limitations You've given me for my own good and well-being. Amen.

Disarmament

A hot-tempered person stirs up conflict, but the one who is patient calms a quarrel.

Proverbs 15:18

Our society has become so unloving that impatience and callousness have become the norm. People are constantly in fight mode. Like a dog that's been kicked and yelled at, they expect to be treated unkindly. In fact, they're shocked when someone does something courteous, merciful, or generous. If the clerk at the checkout line makes a small mistake, she braces herself for the tongue-lashing that's sure to come. If her mistake is quickly forgiven—"No big deal! I probably would have done the same thing"—she's not only surprised; she's intrigued.

Love for one's neighbor, when offered through simple kindness, disarms people. It causes them to let down their defenses, opening the door for Jesus to be part of the conversation.

Want to make a difference in someone's life? Be generous when they're expecting stinginess. Apologize when they're expecting belligerence. Extend mercy when they're expecting accusation. You just might get a chance to tell them about Jesus.

Lord, forgive me for reacting the way the world reacts to minor inconveniences. Help me respond with love and patience instead. Amen.

Through the Eyes of Love

It makes no difference whether you are a Jew or a Greek, a slave or a freeman, a man or a woman, because in Jesus . . . you are all one.

Galatians 3:28 THE VOICE

While dropping off a donation at the shelter, you strike up a conversation with a drifter. You quickly realize you share a passion for fishing, and his knowledge of reels and lures is more extensive than your own. *Wow, we're so much alike!* you think.

Seniors citizens make you uncomfortable, but your best friend drags you to the nursing home. Trying to make the best of it, you say hello to a woman in her nineties and soon discover she has a wicked sense of humor . . . just like you.

Looking at others through the eyes of love allows you to see that the vast differences between you and them aren't really so vast. Then the walls created by an "us and them" mentality come crashing down, and feelings of superiority (*and* inferiority) disintegrate. When we see ourselves in others, we're far less likely to criticize or mistreat them, and love has the last word.

Father, please root the "us and them" mentality out of me. Help me to see that in Jesus, we're all one. Amen.

MARCH

*Know therefore that the LORD your God is God;
he is the faithful God, keeping his covenant of
love to a thousand generations of those who
love him and keep his commandments.*

Deuteronomy 7:9

 # The Curtain

To me, living means living for Christ, and dying is even better.
Philippians 1:21 NLT

There's an old TV show called *My Fair Wedding* that featured a new bride-to-be each episode. The young woman would describe her dream wedding, and for several weeks a collection of people would scramble to pull together the event—plus as many extravagances as possible. Finally, it was time for the unveiling, when the bride would walk through a curtain into a scene that was far more than she could have imagined.

Those who can say, along with Paul, that "dying is even better" than living understand that the partition between this life and the next one is like the curtain on that TV series. Paul knew that leaving this world meant he'd finally be in Jesus' presence forever, in a place of perfect, eternal love. There were times he could barely wait to get there.

For Christians, death loses its sting not because we're suddenly indifferent to it, but because we realize we're simply passing from *life into life*.

Lord, make me ready for the moment when I step through that curtain from this world into perfect, eternal love. Amen.

Holy Mathematics

"'The two will become one flesh.' So they are no longer two, but one flesh."

Mark 10:8

Algebra. Calculus. Geometry.

We use math to explain countless facts because it's ordered and logical. But there are two math equations that can be understood only by the spirit; both concern marriage. The first is *one plus one equals one*. Through marriage, two people become united spiritually, emotionally, physically, and financially. In a very real way, they become a brand-new, single entity.

The other equation is *one plus one equals ten*. Consider that a man who loves God can change the world to a certain extent, and a woman who loves God can also change the world to a certain extent. But together they can share God's love in a way they never could do separately. One person plus one person, united in holy matrimony, can have the impact of ten people acting on their own. This is why we mustn't settle in marriage for just anyone, but for someone with a strong faith.

Thank You, Lord, for the miracle of marriage. May I, and my married friends and family, know the blessing of these two equations. Amen.

Undiluted Christians

"You are the salt of the earth. But what good is salt if it has lost its flavor?"

Matthew 5:13 NLT

Saffron is among the world's most expensive foods because it takes an acre's worth of crocus flowers to produce a single pound. That pound of saffron can cost as much as $10,000![1] Thankfully, however, you don't need much to alter the flavor of a dish. High-quality saffron (which hasn't been diluted with lesser-quality flower parts) is so packed with flavor that just a tiny bit will do the job.

Do you know someone who's like saffron—so packed with the love of God that he or she can speak one timely word and set someone's life on a different course? Or give a hug that's more therapeutic than a thousand ordinary hugs?

God will fill us with His love—He'll keep pouring that love into us as long as we continue to pursue Him. When we keep our passion for God undiluted by the things of this world, His love will inevitably flavor all we do and say.

Lord, I want to be a high-quality Christian, undiluted by the world and seasoning everyone around me with Your love. Amen.

Three Little Questions

A gentle answer deflects anger.

Proverb 15:1 NLT

There are people in our lives we interact with daily . . . but that doesn't mean it's always easy. We all struggle with communicating in a loving way in certain relationships. Is there someone who's an integral part of your life and with whom you'd like to enjoy more harmony and less friction? Each week, ask each other three questions:

1. What is one thing I did this week that made you feel loved or appreciated?
2. What's one thing I did that upset or hurt you?
3. How can I help our relationship in the coming week?

Whether the other person is a relative, friend, or coworker, this exercise can open the way to love. Discuss all three points honestly but gently, allowing the other person to feel safe by refusing to take offense at his or her answers. The potential for cultivating a loving relationship with this exercise is enormous.

Lord, please help me to be a better communicator. May I be honest, gentle, loving, and teachable when discussing things with others. Amen.

Taste and See

Taste and see that the LORD is good. Oh, the joys of those who take refuge in him!

Psalm 34:8 NLT

What's your favorite meal? How about a sizzling, juicy steak, with a steaming baked potato? Or a bowl of pasta and shrimp drowning in melted cheese, with a hunk of crusty bread slathered in butter?

Just as you'd never have to struggle your way through your favorite meal, a relationship with God is meant to be a delight "Taste and see" that God is good, said the psalmist. Loving God is delicious! And He is so good that as you open your heart to Him more and more, He'll enhance and expand every single area of your life. He'll give you a new sense of purpose in your job. He'll increase the unity and joy in your family. He'll be the glue that keeps your marriage together "for better or worse." Even your exercise routine, recreational time, sleep—everything takes on a delicious new life when marinated in the love of God.

Increase my appetite for You, Lord, until I can't go a day without Your presence. Amen.

People Aren't Like Picture Frames

May we never tire of doing what is good and right before our Lord because in His season we shall bring in a great harvest if we can just persist.

Galatians 6:9 THE VOICE

Some people hang on to every memento, every handmade trinket, and their past fifteen years' worth of tax returns. Others are quick to throw things away. Without a second thought, they toss out anything that's unnecessary, broken, or impractical. When it's time to clean the garage, they're virtual tornadoes. This can be a great quality when it comes to keeping a house tidy, but sometimes the "if it's not perfect, trash it" mentality can spread to relationships as well. And when that happens, love becomes conditional.

Maybe you can relate. Perhaps the last time a certain person hurt your feelings, you thought, *I'm over it. She's hurt me for the last time. This friendship is finished.*

Occasionally, we do need to distance ourselves from a relationship, but people aren't disposable, like old picture frames. Don't be too quick to write them off. They're worth loving even when they're broken. After all, that's what God does.

Is there anyone I've prematurely written off as no longer worth the effort, Lord? Please bring them to my remembrance and help me make amends. Amen.

Sharing the Best We Have

Let this be written for a future generation, that a people not yet created may praise the LORD.

When you love someone, you want to share the best you have. "You've got to try this!" you declare, spooning a cheesy blob of lasagna into your son's mouth. "Call a sitter—we're going out tonight," you tell your wife when you get a bonus check.

As Christians, we have the best thing a human being could ever have: the love of God. So we should naturally want to share it. But sermonizing does little to lead people to Jesus. Instead, the most effective way to share God's love is through our gentle words and loving actions. You can talk about forgiving, or you can let it slide the next time someone forgets your birthday. You can preach about giving, or you can hand your daughter the keys to your old car when you purchase a new one.

Share the best you have with those you love—not with a word, but by lavishing on them the same love God lavishes on you.

Your love is the best thing I've ever discovered, Lord! Show me how to share it with those I love. Amen.

The Comparison Game

*For we don't dare classify or compare ourselves with some who
commend themselves. But in measuring themselves by themselves
and comparing themselves to themselves, they lack understanding.*

2 Corinthians 10:12 HCSB

ow-fat! touts the label on a box of microwave popcorn. You're
skeptical: *Low-fat compared to what? A bucket of bacon grease?* You're
right to question the label because there's no standardized way
to measure low-fat versus high-fat when it comes to processed
foods. Take the popcorn company's word for it, and you might
end up frustrated the next time you step on the scale.

When it comes to standards for people, it's tempting to
compare ourselves to others—or others to ourselves. But genuine love doesn't play the comparison game. It's destructive, and
it's also a form of judgment (either the other person comes up
lacking in our estimation, or we decide we're the ones who are
lacking and end up feeling resentful and insecure).

Comparing ourselves to another human being is unloving to both ourselves and the other person. There's only one
standard to measure up to in the kingdom of God, and that's
the loving and forgiving perfection of Jesus Christ.

*Correct me quickly, Lord, any time I start to compare myself to one
of Your other children. Jesus is my standard! Amen.*

Lacking Nothing

"Did you lack anything?"
"Nothing," they answered.

Luke 22:35

Do you feel as if you're waiting for that one thing that'll finally make life complete? *As soon as I snag that promotion . . . as soon as I get my finances squared away . . . as soon as God sends me a spouse . . . as soon as I lose fifteen pounds . . . then life will begin!*

We forget that when we belong to God, when we're recipients of His love, we lack *nothing*. "God has given us everything we need for living a godly life" (2 Peter 1:3 NLT).

Consider Paul: He spent so much time in jail and enduring persecution, he couldn't possibly have been rolling in money. He was single, and according to scholars, he wasn't attractive. Yet he changed the world through the power of his love for God. If his story didn't require a spouse, decent paycheck, great career, or stunning profile, neither does yours. Don't wait—live for God now!

Lord, I worship You, knowing that I'm complete in You. Show me how to live and love for You, just as I am right now. Amen.

God's Not Mad at You

"I will be with you, day after day, to the end of the age."

Matthew 28:20 THE VOICE

I thought you were mad at me."

Has someone you love deeply ever said those words to you because he misinterpreted something you did or said? You probably reassured him, "Of course not! Why would I be mad? Don't you know how much I love you?"

God probably wants to say the same thing to us sometimes. If you've ever experienced a spiritual desert—when it seems God's being very quiet—you know what it's like to wonder if He's angry with you. Times like that can make even veteran Christians feel as if they've somehow driven God away. But He's not fickle, moody, or easily offended, as we humans are. His love is so great that we *can't* drive Him away.

And that spiritual desert? It might not be a desert at all. Those feelings of emptiness and a desire for more might be God's way of inviting you to search for a deeper relationship with Him.

Lord, I trust You're with me right here, right now. I'm so grateful to know that You'll never stop loving me. Amen.

"I Was Just Trying to Be Helpful"

None of you should ever merit suffering like those who have . . .
meddled in the affairs of others or done evil things.

1 Peter 4:15 THE VOICE

A young woman's mother-in-law stops by and immediately starts collecting laundry and loading it into the washer without her daughter-in-law's permission.

To his horror and embarrassment, a young man who's just graduated from college finds out that his dad has shuffled people around at the office to create a job for him.

Both parents were "just trying to be helpful." But are these examples of love, or something else?

Love allows for autonomy. In fact, it rejoices in the individuality of others, honoring their opinions, likes and dislikes, and personal strengths. If you have adult children, resist the urge to treat them as though they're incompetent just because they're younger and less experienced than you. (Remember, they possess skills and talents you might not have.) Don't rush in and save the day. Allow them to learn. If they want your help, they will ask. In the meantime, love them by respecting their rights as adults.

Lord, forgive me for the times I've infringed on others' rights by
helping them without their permission. Amen.

Love Makes You Beautiful

"I dressed you in my splendor and perfected your beauty."

Ezekiel 16:14 NLT

Cosmetics, hair colors, teeth whiteners, liposuction, rhinoplasty, acid peels. Every year, Americans spend astronomical amounts of money trying to look more beautiful. And the number of men who are undergoing surgery for appearance's sake has skyrocketed since the late nineties.

But there's a painless way to take years off your face, and it doesn't cost a cent. "I dressed you in my splendor and perfected your beauty, says the Sovereign LORD." God's love changes us, not just on the inside, but also on the outside. Yes, it's perfectly okay to read that verse in a direct as well as symbolic way! Sin and the shame that comes with it make us look haggard. But "those who look to him are radiant; their faces are never covered with shame" (Psalm 34:5). Another translation reads, "Shame will never contort your faces." (THE VOICE).

From now on, skip the potions and peels. Instead, bask in God's love. It will make you glow inside and out.

Lord, Your love is beautiful. Let it fill me and shine through me so that I am beautiful like You. Amen.

Commitment Issues

God has said, "Never will I leave you; never will I forsake you."
Hebrews 13:5

I used to be married, but I'm much better now, reads a popular meme.

Divorce is so commonplace that we make jokes about it. But the statistics are disheartening. In a recent article, the American Psychological Association reported that 40 to 50 percent of all marriages fail, with the percentage even higher for subsequent marriages.[2] In the meantime, celebrities trade partners faster than they trade cars; and *commitment* has become a vile word to those who value their independence more than they value faithfulness.

Sometimes, our views of the world pollute our spiritual views, and (especially when we've been repeatedly hurt) we equate God's love with what we already know. The result is that we assume He'll eventually abandon us, too, that we'll disappoint Him one too many times. But God doesn't have commitment issues. He won't throw up His hands and finally say, "Enough." God is utterly devoted to us. He's in it not just for the long haul, but *forever.*

Lord, forgive me for assuming You'd eventually leave me as other people have. I put my trust in You and Your everlasting faithfulness. Amen.

Harness the Son

[Jesus] said, "I am the light of the world. Whoever follows me will never walk in darkness, but will have the light of life."

John 8:12

Solar lights work by harnessing the sun. They absorb sunlight, converting it into an electrical current. The electricity charges the batteries and is stored until needed. Eventually, when darkness settles—*voila!*—there's light! After a time, however, the power will be depleted, until the sun reappears.

If you're a Christ follower, you're just like that solar light. When you step into the Lord's presence, the love of God soaks in—which empowers you—and out comes the power of joy, wisdom, kindness, patience, and more.

Life's millions of trials and labors will drain that power unless you consistently soak up God's love. You simply won't function as you should without spending time with Him. Yes, you can run on reserves for a short time, but soon you'll be utterly depleted. Nothing absorbed equals nothing to give.

If you're feeling depressed, exhausted, irritable, impatient, or fearful, recharge by taking time to soak up the love of God.

You're my only source of pure light, Lord. Thank You for being the Lamp that lights my path. Amen.

Don't Give Up

The Spirit of God has made me; the breath of the Almighty gives me life.

Job 33:4

Depending on where you live, you might already be seeing signs of spring. Maybe you're itching to get outside and do some landscaping. But be warned: every year, some well-intentioned gardener makes the mistake of cutting down a small tree or bush too soon. They assume it's dead because it remains leafless when everything around it is blooming, but all it needed was a bit more time, a few more days in the sun, and it would have burst with color and fragrance and life.

Some people are like these little trees and bushes: slow to show signs of new life, but worth waiting for. Is there someone to whom you've been witnessing for a long time with no success? Are you about to give up? Hold on a little longer. Be persistent in showering God's love on that stubborn unbeliever, and you might discover he's simply a late bloomer.

Lord, don't let me give up on those who don't seem to be responding to the gospel. Help me remember that You want everyone to come to You (2 Peter 3:9). Amen.

Sing a Psalm

I will sing and make music to the LORD.

Psalm 27:6

Have you ever been driving down the road while listening to an oldies station when a favorite song from high school came on and suddenly you were singing the words from memory—without missing a beat? Many people can recall all the words to the *Gilligan's Island* theme song, "A Whole New World," or "Bohemian Rhapsody," even after decades. Why? Because people retain information better and longer when it's sung rather than spoken.

We have one 150 songs, called psalms, in the Bible. Granted, we don't know the melodies anymore, but we can certainly add our own. Maybe you're one of the many Christians who truly loves the Word but has trouble with memorization. If so, pick a favorite psalm and sing it however you wish. Or choose a Christian song that features words from a psalm. God doesn't mind if your voice isn't perfect or your rhythm is a bit off beat. He just loves to hear you sing His Word!

Lord, lead me to the psalm that's most fitting for my life right now, and then give me a melody to sing it. Amen.

When You Don't Feel Like It

What does the LORD your God require of you? . . . Love him and serve him with all your heart and soul.

Deuteronomy 10:12 NLT

A father is repeatedly disappointed by his teenager's decisions. He loves his daughter, but sometimes it's hard to like her. In the ebb and flow of a long marriage, a wife is experiencing a time when her husband feels far away.

Both of these are normal situations in which people may not *feel* especially loving, even though they love the other person. But whether or not we *do* the loving thing can't be dependent on how someone makes us feel; feelings come and go. When our love is in line with Jesus' example, our behavior will conform, whether we've got the warm fuzzies or not.

Our love for God must be the same. Sometimes we'll experience our love for Him in our emotions, but other times we won't. In those moments, we'll show our love through our obedience. We'll keep the faith not because we feel like it, but simply because we belong to Him.

Sometimes I don't feel very loving, Lord. When that happens, please know that I do still love You, and help me to show You my love through my actions. Amen.

Come Inside

This is what the Lord has commanded us: "I have made you a light for the Gentiles, that you may bring salvation to the ends of the earth."

Acts 13:47

Why does a fireplace feel extra cozy during a snowfall? Why is our bed so snuggly when thunder booms and lightning flashes? The reason is that fireplaces and warm beds remind us that we're not "out there." They make the pleasure of being inside versus outside that much more enjoyable. The trouble, however, is that some people are still out there, homeless and unprotected even in the storms.

The Christian's refuge is the love of God. Inside the fortress of His love, we can feel secure, cared for, and peaceful. But the tragedy is that many, many people are still "out there." They ache to be inside God's love, even if they don't understand what they're longing for. Without the sanctuary that God provides through Jesus, they won't survive. It's up to us to invite them in.

Are you sheltered by the love of God? If not, will you come in? And if so, are you inviting others inside?

Thank You, Lord, for inviting me to find shelter inside Your love. There's no place quite as cozy! Amen.

Squeaky Doors

As vinegar vexes the teeth, and as smoke irritates the eyes, so a slacker annoys his boss.

Proverbs 10:26 THE VOICE

A curtain rod that falls every time you open the window. That pair of shoes that always make your heels ache. The bedroom door that squeaks. Sometimes the smallest annoyances cause far more stress than they should, considering they could be easily remedied. That faulty curtain rod might need nothing more than a new screw—a two-minute task—yet so easy to put off.

Sometimes we do the same thing in our relationships with those we love: we let a tiny annoyance cause unnecessary conflict simply because we don't stop, identify it, and make necessary changes. For example, if you find yourself angry and frustrated with your kids every evening because they won't stop checking their phones during dinner, taking a few minutes to institute a no-phones-at-the-table policy could offer a huge payoff.

Have you been annoyed with a loved one lately? Ask God to show you how to remedy the situation in love.

Lord, please help me to stop procrastinating and make the minor adjustments that would cut down on conflicts. Amen.

Gongs and Cymbals

If I speak in the tongues of men or of angels, but do not have love, I am only a resounding gong or a clanging cymbal.

1 Corinthians 13:1

Have you ever struck a gong or crashed a pair of cymbals together? If so, you probably noticed they make a racket, but they can't create a melody. They don't produce music, per se—just noise. In the world of music and instruments, they do the least communicating. They can actually become annoying very quickly, much like the beeping of a fire alarm with low batteries, or the relentless *woof-woof-woof* of a neighbor's dog. It's only when these instruments are backed up by others that they sound like music.

Like crashing cymbals, our faith, words, and actions must be backed up by the melody of love. Paul explained that even if we speak the language of the angels, our words will amount to nothing but noise if we're unloving.

If our lives, our words, and our actions aren't rooted in love, then—like those crashing cymbals—we'll annoy people at best and turn them away from the Lord's love at worst.

I want to be far, far more than an annoying gong or clanging cymbal, Lord. Please fill my life with the melody of Your flawless love. Amen.

Our Accessible God

"You will seek me and find me when you seek me with all your heart."
Jeremiah 29:13

The presence and love of God is sometimes more apparent and more powerful in a young child or a mentally challenged individual than in the most educated and articulate Christian. The reason for this is that even though God's love and presence are profound, the way into that love and presence is profoundly *simple*.

God is completely accessible. He's "user-friendly" and always available. Finding God's love is not complicated; therefore, offering His love to others should never be complicated either. A person doesn't need to be grown-up, sinless, educated, clever, healthy, successful, or refined to tap into God. She can be young, wayward, uneducated, naive, sick, unsuccessful, and uncultured, but God will quickly reveal Himself through her as long as she's willing. When it comes to sharing God's love, keep it simple.

Thank You, Lord, for making it so simple to tap into Your love and offer it to others. Amen.

Love: The Purest Motive

If I gave everything I have to the poor and even sacrificed my body, I could boast about it; but if I didn't love others, I would have gained nothing.

1 Corinthians 13:3 NLT

Today's verse cautions us against doing the right things for all the wrong reasons. Giving to the poor and even surrendering to martyrdom gains us nothing, if we don't have the love of God in our hearts. Many good things are done by people who don't love God. There have always been those who appear virtuous but who have wrong motives.

So how can we be sure that our righteous deeds are truly counted as righteous, and that, in the end, they do matter? It all boils down to love, Paul explained. Love of God and love for others. Just think: in the currency of heaven, that million-dollar donation from the unbelieving philanthropist counts as nothing when compared to the teenager who babysits her neighbor's kids for free simply to show the love of Jesus.

What compels you to volunteer at the animal shelter, slip an extra fifty dollars into the love offering, or head up VBS each summer? Is it love for the Lord? Is it love for His children? Then do it with joy!

Help me, Lord, to take a look at my good works and make sure they're backed up by a life that's built on love. Amen.

When There's More Than One Right Way

The one who has knowledge uses words with restraint, and whoever has understanding is even-tempered.

Proverbs 17:27

"I wear jeans and a T-shirt to church because I'm not legalistic," you say (in front of a woman who enjoys dressing to the nines on Sundays).

"I'd never send my kids to public school. I homeschool," you boast (in front of the mom with six kids in public school).

Sometimes we forget that our way isn't necessarily the *only* right way. Often there are several acceptable ways to do something. But we tend to take pride in *our* way and deem it the most virtuous option, which can cause us to offend our brothers and sisters.

We must be careful not to profess to love people while doing and saying things that communicate, "You are, if only marginally, inferior to me, and I want to make sure that you and everyone else knows it." Remember, love doesn't boast, strut about, or cause division. It doesn't strive to have the last say or put others in their place. Love . . . loves.

Help me, Lord, to watch my words and attitudes. Forgive me for boasting and believing that my way is the only right way. Amen.

The Genuine People Person

Never let loyalty and kindness leave you! . . . Then you will find favor with both God and people, and you will earn a good reputation.

Proverbs 3:3–4 NLT

Are you a "people person"?

If you're naturally an introvert, you might be tempted to say no, since most introverts need to limit the amount of time they spend making small talk, or being with crowds of people, or playing the social butterfly. But being a people person doesn't necessarily mean relishing social events, having seventy-five close friends, or even being a fantastic conversationalist.

Shouldn't the term *people person* be defined as "someone who loves people"? In the truest sense, then, a people person recognizes that every person on earth has great value, that all life is sacred, and that human beings are created in God's image. A people person treats others with dignity and honor and extends simple kindnesses, such as not interrupting. She's able to empathize with the wounded and laugh with the joyful. He's willing to love in a way that's constant, honest, and sacrificial. So . . . are you a people person?

Dear Lord, I want to be a people person in the purest sense of the word. Teach me how to do so. Amen.

Landscaping

A person's wisdom yields patience; it is to one's glory to overlook an offense.

Few things add to a home's curb appeal like lovely landscaping. But it takes attention and consistent maintenance. After all, no boxwood has ever trimmed itself into a perfectly flat-topped hedge to save you the trouble. Ignoring the landscaping in your yard quickly turns little bushes into gangly trees. What should have required a thirty-dollar pair of hedge shears now seems impossible without a chainsaw.

Much like a neglected hedge, small offenses and grudges can grow rapidly and get out of control before you know it. Sometimes they can become monstrous overnight, running wild and swiftly becoming very hard to trim. The key is to lop them off immediately. Give them no time to get tough and dense and difficult to cut back.

The next time someone upsets you, and you realize you're about to take offense, waste no time. Be proactive. Choose to forgive. Choose to love.

Please give me the inner strength, Lord, to nip offense in the bud before it has a chance to grow. Thank You! Amen.

Set Your Thoughts on Jesus

Don't let anyone capture you with empty philosophies and high-sounding nonsense that come from human thinking . . . rather than from Christ.

Colossians 2:8 NLT

Maybe you've decided that many problems in this world are a result of people not loving themselves enough. But the issue isn't exactly with loving ourselves. In a way, we already do too much of that! We all struggle with selfishness and setting ourselves above others. But at the same time, many of us also wrestle with self-hatred. We end up swinging like a pendulum between putting our own needs above the needs of others and engaging in self-loathing.

So which is it? Should we be more focused on ourselves—or less? Neither! Our focus should be on Jesus alone. With Him at the forefront of our minds, we won't think of ourselves too highly *or* too critically. We'll see ourselves through God's eyes and according to His truth, not our own opinions. And the truth is that, though we're broken and weak apart from Him, we are priceless to Him.

Lord, I choose to set my eyes on You, not on myself. Show me who I am in You. Amen.

Love Your Neighbor

"Love your neighbor as yourself."

What did Jesus mean by, "Love your neighbor as yourself"? Most of us would agree that we give a lot of thought to our needs and desires, and that we usually strive to meet those needs as quickly as possible. Jesus was simply telling us to do the same for others.

Imagine someone who can't stand being cold. As soon as winter arrives, she starts counting the days until spring. She turns the thermostat up to 78 degrees and wiggles into so many layers before going outside that she can barely move. If it's important to this woman to fulfill Matthew 22:39, she might collect coats and blankets and then head up a giveaway at her church. She'll think, *I can't imagine anything worse than being cold all winter, and I won't stand for anyone else being cold either!* Her need for warmth will translate into action on behalf of others. *That* is loving your neighbor as yourself.

Lord, teach me to give as much thought to meeting the needs of my neighbors as I do to meeting my own needs. Amen.

Overboard

Enoch had such a close and intimate relationship with God that one day he just vanished—God took him.

Genesis 5:24 THE VOICE

Some things require restraint or moderation. Sugar, for instance. No one ever ended up obese by enjoying a bit of sugar on special occasions, but three sodas a day can have terrible consequences. Exercise, sleep, entertainment—all these things are great, but only to a point.

Does the same apply to loving God? Can we go overboard in our love for Him? If we were to grow daily in genuine love for Him, what might happen? Maybe that is what happened to Enoch—he became so intertwined with God that the next step was absolute union with Him, and he vanished into God's heart.

When it comes to loving God, there's no point in restraint. He's never greeted anyone in heaven by saying, "Well done, faithful servant, but you went slightly overboard in your love for Me." Go ahead, and love God with everything you are!

Lord, never let it be said of me that I loved You in moderation.
Spark a fire in me that will never fade. Amen.

Err on the Side of Grace

The righteous give and don't hold back.

Proverbs 21:26 HCSB

Just as it's impossible to go overboard in your love for God, it's impossible to genuinely love your neighbor to excess.

The love of God is perfect and balanced. It's never tainted by insecurity, jealousy, fear, or other dysfunctions, as our imperfect, human love sometimes is. Therefore, when we allow God to love people through us, we always hit our mark.

But what should we do when we suspect our humanness is getting in the way? For example, should we give that person who hurt us one more chance? Should we loan our financially strapped friend $100? In these instances, is saying yes loving or enabling bad behavior?

Try this rule of thumb: If the Lord seems to be prompting you to do a certain thing, obey immediately. But if you're truly unsure, err on the side of grace. If you later discover you goofed, you'll have the comfort of knowing your motive was love.

Please speak to me loudly and clearly, Lord, but if I still don't hear You accurately, may I err on the side of grace. Amen.

Do What You Love

His word is in my heart like a fire, a fire shut up in my bones. I am weary of holding it in; indeed, I cannot.

Jeremiah 20:9

Have you ever heard, "If it tastes great, it's probably bad for you"? Since we tend to love the foods that clog our arteries, we often associate "pleasurable" with "bad for me."

Sometimes we make the same association regarding ministry. We assume that if we enjoy doing something, it can't possibly be our calling. Doesn't serving God require difficulty, unpleasantness, and sacrifice? Not at all!

What's your passion? Is there something you simply must do, or you'll shrivel up inside? Maybe you love to sculpt. If you also love the Lord, it's very likely that your sculptures reflect that love because our gifts and passions are designed to communicate God's love to others. Athlete Eric Liddell believed it was God who made him fast and that to run was pleasing to God. Because Eric loved God and running, the two were deeply intertwined. Whatever you love doing the most, thank God for it, and do it for His glory.

Lord, thank You so much for the joy I feel when I _____. May I communicate Your love through this gift You've given me. Amen.

Innocent

What joy for those whose record the LORD has cleared of guilt.

Psalm 32:2 NLT

et's face it: crime shows are great fun to watch. We sit on the edge of our seats as the good guys build a case against the suspect. Bit by bit, they find pieces of evidence—a splotch of blood, an incriminating e-mail, a trace of DNA. Finally, everything comes crashing down around the bad guy. By the end of the show, he's behind bars where he belongs.

Unfortunately, some people view God as the Good Guy who's building a case against them—even many Christians whose slates have been wiped clean. They struggle to believe God truly sees them as innocent. Other folks spend a great deal of time building a case against themselves: *My whole life is a failure; I'll never measure up; I'm such a loser.*

One glimpse of God's true love would bring all that to a screeching halt. God's *not* the great Prosecutor—He's the One who sets us free!

Forgive me, Lord, for the time and energy I've wasted feeling guilty when You see me as innocent! Amen.

APRIL

So may all your enemies perish, Lord! But may all
who love you be like the sun when it rises in its strength.

Judges 5:31

A Mess or a Message?

He will give a crown of beauty for ashes, a joyous blessing instead of mourning, festive praise instead of despair.

Isaiah 61:3 NLT

When Bill Wilson was twelve, his mother left him on a street corner and never returned. He waited at that intersection for three days until a Christian gentleman noticed him and picked him up. Shortly after, Bill was saved at a Sunday school camp. He eventually became the founder of Metro World Child, which shares God's love with thousands of children all over the world through fun, hands-on Sunday school programs and kids' camps.[1]

It's been said that the love of God can take our mess and turn it into our greatest message. Bill Wilson allowed God to take the deep rejection he had experienced from his mother and mold it into a life of deep love that has changed many, many lives.

Has the devil made a mess in your life? Or have you created the mess yourself? Either way, God can transform it into a message of hope, restoration, and love. Will you let Him?

You know the mess in my life, Lord. I offer it to You now. Please take it from me and mold it into Your message. Amen.

The Spark That Brings Hardship

"Go into all the world and preach the gospel to all creation."

Mark 16:15

If we think "go[ing] into all the world" means embarking on an exciting journey filled with world travel and status, we're sadly mistaken. Those who spend their lives loving the poor and unsaved know all about sacrifice and self-denial and even danger. Consider the missionary Jim Eliot. In 1956, he was killed by the very people he was serving—the Huaorani people of Ecuador. He hadn't even reached his thirtieth birthday![2]

In a perfect world, being a Christian would mean protection from any kind of suffering. Salvation would be our ticket out of pain and hardship and into an easy-breezy life. But the fact is, even though most Americans will never be killed for their beliefs, sharing the message of Jesus and the love of God with others can actually be the spark that brings hardship into our lives!

So why put ourselves out there? Because sharing the life-changing gospel of Jesus is worth the hardship.

I understand, Lord, that sharing You with the world means sacrifice and risk, but You're worth it! Please give me the courage to "go into all the world." Amen.

Sharing Our Struggles

Do not be anxious about anything, but in every situation, by prayer and petition, with thanksgiving, present your requests to God.

Philippians 4:6

Have you ever greeted someone new with "How are you?" and then that person spent twenty minutes telling you his deepest secrets? If so, you probably scrambled for a way to escape. We aren't comfortable when someone tells all before we've forged a friendship. Neither do we want to bear our own souls to someone we barely know.

But it's a different story when it comes to our closest friends. We don't mind hearing their secrets, and confiding in them brings relief because we know they love us in spite of our troubles. In describing one of his closest friendships, Henri Nouwen said, "The sharing of our deep struggles became a sign of our friendship."[3]

Jesus is the truest Friend you can have. Do you share your deep struggles with Him? Are you comfortable telling Him everything? If not, dare to take your friendship to the next level.

Thank You for being that Friend who loves me through thick and thin, and the One I can trust with all my secrets. Amen.

Try a Little Kindness

Love is kind.

1 Corinthians 13:4

ave you ever cringed when listening to some people—who supposedly love one another—talk to each other?

"What were you thinking?"

"You're such an idiot."

"You're driving me nuts!"

Kindness is a simple word, but it's packed with power. It can tear down walls and set things right between parent and child, friend and friend, or husband and wife in a way that few other things can. Yet it's lacking in many relationships. In our often hostile world, we've lost the art of being kind.

Are your relationships seasoned with kindness? You might think that cutting or sarcastic remark will convince a person to shape up and do things your way, but you're actually damaging your relationship. (And following an insult with "Just kidding" doesn't let you off the hook!) Stop buying into the lie that spitefulness is acceptable. Commit to an attitude of loving-kindness, and see what happens in your home, workplace, and church.

Bring to my remembrance times that I've been unkind to someone, Lord, and help me restore that relationship with kindness. Amen.

Love and Anxiety

Since God cares for you, let Him carry all your burdens and worries.
1 Peter 5:7 THE VOICE

How's your daughter adjusting to college?"

"She seems to be doing well, but I can barely sleep from worrying about her!"

"I'm sure you *do* worry. How could you *not*?"

Most of us would agree that fear isn't God's will for us. Even so, we'd make an exception in a case like this or something similar, such as a friend being hospitalized or going through a divorce. Surely it's okay to feel fearful then, right? What would it say about us if we didn't?

Often, we equate love with worry. Some parents would find it impossible to stop fretting about their adult children without also feeling like terrible parents. But when you love someone, you're *not* required to agonize over his or her well-being. Instead, you're instructed to entrust him or her to God's care. It's wonderful to pray for your loved ones and help however you can, but love of the purest kind is flavored with faith, not fear.

Lord, deliver me from the lie that caring for others means I must worry about them. I place my loved ones in Your perfect care. Amen.

Be Still

Let all that I am wait quietly before God.

Psalm 62:5 NLT

*I*magine you're planning a trip to a location several hours away when a friend suggests you carpool with someone she knows. "He's making the same trip and wouldn't mind splitting the gas with you." Does the thought of a road trip with a virtual stranger make you uncomfortable? If so, it's probably because you'd feel obligated to make conversation the whole way. After all, long silences can be excruciating, and filling up dead air with chatter is exhausting.

In solid, long-term relationships, however, sitting in silence without a trace of awkwardness is normal. Old friends, spouses, and cherished relatives don't require constant chitchat because love means the freedom to be still. God wants you to be as comfortable sitting quietly in His presence as you are with your favorite people. This is why stillness is a spiritual discipline worth learning. If you struggle to be still with God, ask Him to calm your spirit and to teach you how.

When I try too hard to fill my day with activity and chatter, slow me down, Lord. Teach me to be still in Your presence. Amen.

The Person You Don't Want to See

Be kind and compassionate to one another, forgiving each other, just as in Christ God forgave you.

Fill in the blank below with the name of someone you know:

When I get to heaven, I'll be really mad/shocked/disappointed if I find out that _____ is there too.

Did a particular person come to mind? How did you feel when you thought about him or her? Were you upset at the idea that God might love that person enough to let him or her into heaven? If so, is it possible you have hard feelings, even bitterness, toward this person?

Sometimes we assume God would never extend forgiveness to someone who's offended us—as if that's the unforgivable sin! If the idea of sharing your eternal home with a certain person irritates or angers you, it's a good sign you need to examine your heart for unforgiveness. With the Holy Spirit's help, you *can* release your anger, choose to love that person, and then move on . . . with a pure heart.

With Your eyes of love, Lord, look into my heart and tell me if there's anyone I need to forgive. Then help me to release that person once and for all. Amen.

God Knows

"Before I formed you in the womb I knew you."

Jeremiah 1:5

Driving or even walking in fog can be disconcerting or even downright scary. Most of us know that shivery feeling of fear that something—or, worse yet, some*one*—will pop up unexpectedly in front of us. In cases like this, no one likes to be taken by surprise.

God is never taken by surprise. No fog ever obscures His vision. He knows what's going to happen to you in the next minute *and* twenty years from now. As today's verse says, He even knew you before you were born. There's nothing you can do, nothing that can happen to you, that will catch God off guard. And He already has the answer to any situation you might encounter.

God's love for you is so deep, so wide, and so high that He can be totally trusted to guide, protect, and rescue you. Facing a big problem? Take it to Him. God *is* the answer.

Father God, teach me to trust You for the answers to all my problems. I know You already have the perfect answers. Amen.

On the Altar

Moses then took all the offerings . . . and burned them on the altar. . . . It was a pleasing aroma, a special gift presented to the Lord.

Leviticus 8:28 NLT

Wouldn't it be wonderful to be "a pleasing aroma" and a "special gift" to God? We *can* be, if we love Him and are willing to offer our lives to His service. We can lay ourselves on the altar, so to speak, and die to all our selfish desires and plans. We can allow Him to burn up everything in our hearts that's displeasing to Him. He longs to strip us of everything that keeps us separated from Him—not because He's cruel, but because He loves us so much He wants us for Himself.

Most of us have to fight the impulse to jump down off that altar. We want to take control of our lives again and do things our own way. This is why offering ourselves as special gifts to the Lord has to be a daily decision.

Have you offered yourself—the bad *and* the good—to God today?

Lord, show me how to climb up on the altar and give You everything I am. I belong to You! Amen.

Be Patient

*There was a time when we were like children held under the
elemental powers of this world.*

Galatians 4:3 THE VOICE

*I*f you're a veteran Christian, you've probably discovered that
it's most difficult to be patient with someone who reminds
you of your younger self. If you struggled with lying as an
immature believer, you probably have all kinds of grace for
other sins—but you have zero tolerance for lying.

Loving the body of Christ, however, means being patient
and generous with those who are less mature than you are . . .
even if they remind you of yourself! Don't forget where you
came from. There was probably a time when you fumbled
through your walk with Christ, tripped over the most funda-
mental doctrines, and slipped quickly back into old habits.

On the other hand, if you're a "newbie" to the faith or to
ministry, don't resent those who know more than you. They're
paving the way, making mistakes so you don't have to. Respect
them, love them, and appreciate the wisdom they pass on to you.

*Thank You, Lord, for the young believers who are growing daily.
Help me to guide them with patience. Amen.*

Love and Sacrifice

Live in love as the Anointed One loved you—so much that He gave Himself as a fragrant sacrifice, pleasing God.

Ephesians 5:2 THE VOICE

When you hear the word *worship*, do you think about your favorite song or last Sunday's church service? Those things are certainly part of worship, and yet when we read about worship in the Old Testament, we see rituals that seem nearly barbaric: animals on an altar, slaughter, blood, fire! This is because worship meant sacrifice, which went hand in hand with death. Bulls, doves, and lambs were laid on an altar, and then the whole lot was burned to produce a fragrance that would please the Lord.

With the arrival of Jesus, the meaning behind this sacrifice became clear: Jesus was the perfect sacrificial Lamb, sent to earth by a Father who loves us beyond measure. Jesus' death was brutal and bloody, but it was the only thing that could bring us back to God. This is why He so deserves our devotion. How wonderful that our worship produces a fragrance that pleases Him.

Father, thank You for loving me enough to send Jesus. And Jesus, thank You for loving me enough to endure the cross. Amen.

Loving the Ordinary Things

Whatever you do, work at it with all your heart, as working for the Lord.

Colossians 3:23

"The honeymoon's over!" someone says as the newly married couple settles into the ordinary, everyday efforts of life. Wouldn't it be lovely to experience the high of new love every single day? But even the best marriage must include daily rituals and chores, or else life grinds to a halt.

Similarly, the God-life should have its highs, but it must also include certain daily disciplines and efforts. Some days, Bible reading or visiting a sick friend might feel like a chore. But don't let the everyday duties and routines weigh you down; instead, let them serve as a sturdy foundation for your faith. Those daily disciplines, if done from a place of loving commitment, are the very things that will see you through the lows until your reach the next spiritual high. As you set about your daily chores, remind yourself: *This task is a privilege. I'm happy to do it as part of the family of God!*

Lord, help me to be appreciative and joyful while carrying out the daily chores of this awesome life You've given me. Amen.

Plenty of God to Go Around

We know how dearly God loves us, because he has given us the Holy Spirit to fill our hearts with his love.

Romans 5:5 NLT

If you grew up with siblings, you probably said at one time or another, "You love him more than you love me!" And your parents probably rolled their eyes and then reassured you that they had plenty of love to go around.

Sadly, some believers never outgrow their feelings of insecurity. Year after year, they continue to wonder where they stand in relation to everyone else on God's "love scale." They search for evidence that they're loved as much as their brothers and sisters in Christ, forgetting that God *is* love, and therefore He has an infinite supply of love to give.

Although it sounds silly, sometimes it needs to be said: there's plenty of God to go around. The fact that He's madly in love with the person standing next to you in the church pew doesn't diminish the fact that He's also—and ever will be— madly in love with you.

Remove every bit of insecurity from me, Lord, and teach me so that I never have to doubt how much You love me. Amen.

Adoption and Inheritance

The Spirit you received brought about your adoption to sonship.
And by him we cry, "Abba, Father."

Romans 8:15

"A son or daughter . . . is either born to or adopted by the parents," said author Jerry Bridges. "By definition, a child can't be both. But with God we're both *born of* Him and *adopted by* Him."[4]

God tells us that He's adopted us. We didn't earn the status of sons and daughters, but God has granted it anyway . . . simply because He loves us so completely.

At the time today's verse was written, adoption took place in front of seven officials. If the child had any rights and responsibilities—*or* debts and obligations—in connection with his former family, they were cancelled. Once the adoption was complete, he had the same opportunities, benefits, and responsibilities as a natural-born child. And though a biological child could be disinherited, an adopted child could not. His inheritance was sure. That means *you* are a co-heir with Christ (Romans 8:17)—and your inheritance is sure!

Abba, Father! I believe with all my heart that I'm forever Yours.
Amen.

Gone for Good

The Egyptians tried to escape, but the Lord swept them into the sea. Then the waters returned and covered all the chariots and charioteers—the entire army of Pharaoh. . . . Not a single one survived.

Exodus 14:27–28 NLT

Many people who lose weight gain it back, *plus* a few extra pounds. Former addicts often revert to their drug of choice when faced with a crisis. As human beings, we tend to slip back into negative behavior, especially when life gets stressful.

But that doesn't have to be our story. God offers hope to those who look to Him while trying to overcome their issues. He wants us to be free of the things that harm us—not just for a while, but for good.

Isn't it presumptuous to think that we can be free forever when the statistics say differently? Not at all. Remember how the Israelites crossed the Red Sea? God split the waters. Then, once His children had all crossed, the Egyptians followed in hot pursuit—so God released the water, which swallowed up the enemy: "Not a single one survived."

God doesn't do things halfway. His love will swallow up fear, addiction, and brokenness—forever!

Swallow up the enemy in my life, Lord. Free me to forever live in Your love. Amen.

Garbage?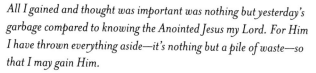

All I gained and thought was important was nothing but yesterday's garbage compared to knowing the Anointed Jesus my Lord. For Him I have thrown everything aside—it's nothing but a pile of waste—so that I may gain Him.

Philippians 3:8 THE VOICE

Was Paul being extreme when he referred to the things he'd once considered important as *garbage* (also translated *filth*, *rubbish*, or even *dung*)? Wasn't that a little harsh? Surely his education, status, and associates didn't constitute "a pile of waste." But Paul had discovered that *everything* in his life was expendable in order to gain Jesus. He was like the man who sold everything to buy the treasure hidden in a field (Matthew 13:44). There was likely nothing inherently wrong with that man's possessions, but the treasure was infinitely better.

The things that Paul had "gained and thought [were] important" might not have been bad things—they were probably good things—but the love of Jesus was so much better, that to compare them would have been almost comical. Therefore, he used the word *garbage*—an in-your-face, slightly scandalous word—to describe the things he'd forfeited to secure Jesus. Because next to His presence and love, everything else is worthless.

Lord, nothing compares to You. Help me to let go of anything that stands in the way of my love for You. Amen.

Do for One

Do you have the gift of helping others? Do it with all the strength and energy that God supplies.

1 Peter 4:11 NLT

For fifty-two years, Carlos Arredondo was no more famous than the average person. But in April 2013, someone snapped his photo as he wheeled twenty-seven-year-old Jeff Bauman from the carnage of the Boston Marathon bombing toward an ambulance. Today, millions recognize Arredondo's face because, in the midst of immense suffering, he saw one particular need and chose to do something about it. As a result, he saved a life.[5]

Maybe you've wished you could help everyone everywhere, only to discover there's not enough of you to go around. This realization paralyzes some, prompting them to give up because there's just too much suffering in the world. But as Pastor Andy Stanley has said, "Do for one what you wish you could do for everyone."[6] Focus on *one* person and *one* need. Then, take a step toward meeting that need. Do the same tomorrow, and the next day, and the next. You just might save a life.

Lord, show me that one person I can help today. Tomorrow and the next day and each day after that, please do the same. Amen.

What Is Love?

Let love be genuine. Abhor what is evil; hold fast to what is good.

Romans 12:9 ESV

Because we toss the word *love* around so casually (and because we're broken and wounded human beings), we tend to call certain things *love* that don't deserve that label by any stretch of the imagination. For example, a friend tends to gravitate toward boyfriends who are overly jealous and controlling because she mistakenly believes this is their way of showing how much they love her.

Even the most emotionally healthy person probably has some misconceptions about love. Only God can truly straighten out our understanding of what love truly is and what it isn't. So if you realize your definition of love is associated with something dysfunctional or dangerous or sinful, turn to God and His Word. Let Him define what love really is. He'll show you how to separate the good from the bad, and He'll teach you what's pure and true. For He *is* love.

Dear Lord, I know I have some wrong ideas about what constitutes love; please help me to separate truth from error. Amen.

Outdo One Another

Love one another with brotherly affection. Outdo one another in showing honor.

Romans 12:10 ESV

Really great marriages often have a few common denominators. One is that both partners go out of their way to treat the other with respect and kindness. In fact, you might say that some couples make a game of out spoiling one another. For example, if a husband loves to cook, he might delight in making his wife feel like a queen by fixing her meals that are healthy, beautiful, and delicious. She, in turn, might pamper him by shooing him into the TV room afterward so he doesn't wash a single dish.

Our society is so fixated on self that the idea of a spouse striving to give more than he or she receives will make some people uncomfortable. "You do for me, and *then* I'll do for you," is the typical mind-set. But that's not how Jesus loves us. And we'll never go wrong by attempting to love our spouses as He loves us.

Father, You go way out of Your way to love me! Help me to do the same for the people in my life. Amen.

Unplugged

They were talking with each other about everything that had happened.

Luke 24:14

More and more people are learning the value of taking a break from electronics. This can range from turning off one's phone after a certain hour or when eating meals to getting rid of the TV altogether.

Many individuals have found—to their delight—that the result of putting limits on their interaction with electronics is that they actually start talking to other human beings! Without Facebook and sitcoms to arrest their attention, they discuss their day, their problems, and their aspirations with friends and family. They trade their typical evening routine (staring at a screen) for activities they enjoy even more. In this way, they nurture and strengthen their friendships, improve their health by getting off the couch and moving, and rediscover old pastimes, such as reading books made of real paper. It's not always an easy transition, but ask yourself: are the people and the God you love worth more than your gadgets?

Give me the determination, Lord, to sacrifice whatever gadgets need to go in order to strengthen myself and my relationships. Amen.

Choosing Your Battles

"Blessed are the merciful, for they will be shown mercy."

Matthew 5:7

We've all heard the saying, "Choose your battles," but sometimes we forget to apply it in our own lives.

Think about something a family member, friend, or colleague does that makes you *crazy*. Maybe your teenager drops his dirty clothes two inches from the laundry basket. Or maybe your best friend has *never* remembered your birthday. Give your friend a gift, instead, by letting him off the hook. Make a commitment to remember that because this person is flawed (as are you), you won't count that thing against him. It'll no longer be a point of contention. Instead, you'll accept his flaws as a small price to pay for the privilege of having him in your life.

Choosing your battles requires patience and humility, but if you can learn to do it, you'll find you have less stress and more energy to focus on the relationship, making it better for you both.

Lord, You know my struggles with other people. Show me which battles I need to let go of to foster love. Amen.

Curse or Blessing?

The cooing of doves is heard in our land.

Song of Songs 2:12

Spring is here! It's time to plant flowers. But be warned: if you opt for zinnias, you'll get goldfinches, too. Goldfinches are gorgeous little birds, but they love zinnias and will pluck the petals off every flower in just a few days. When that happens, you have a choice: you can see the goldfinches as a lovely little gifts from God, or a nuisance. You can try to chase the birds away and miss out on their charm and beauty. *Or* you can set out a goldfinch feeder, which will save your flowers and grant you a double blessing.

Many of the best things often have a few drawbacks. Do you choose to see the gifts of a loving God, or do you focus on the parts that annoy you? For example, do you think of summer as the season for swimming and flip-flops—or sunburn and sweltering heat? When there are two ways to look at a thing, choose to see the loving gift—and your blessings will automatically multiply.

Lord, give me eyes that are quick to see beauty and blessings and slow to see annoyances. Amen.

Submit Your Weakness

Submit to one another out of reverence for Christ.

Ephesians 5:21

Like it or not, submission is part of loving others. There are many ways to submit to others, but consider this one: *submit your weaknesses to the strengths of other people.* What does this mean? It means that if you've been the office party planner for years because no one else would do it, but the newbie has a real knack for it, consider letting her take over. If your wife is great at handling money, and you'd rather fold a thousand fitted sheets than balance a checkbook, let her create the family budget.

The same principle applies to strength and weakness in character. Are you quickly tempted to dive into gossip, while you've never heard your best friend slander anyone? Then be quick to listen when she cautions you against bashing your boss.

Sometimes, submission means allowing your loved ones to be strong while you lean on *and* learn from them.

Lord, thank You for putting people into my life who are strong where I'm weak. I choose to submit to and learn from them. Amen.

Color

"Make the tabernacle with ten curtains of finely twisted linen and blue, purple and scarlet yarn."

Exodus 26:1

Imagine a world without color. From the time you woke up in the morning until you went to sleep at night, all you could see were shades of black, grey, and white. What would your child look like? A field of wildflowers? A sunset?

God created this world, and though He knew full well we'd be a "rebellious and stiff-necked" people (Deuteronomy 31:27), He chose to give us a world of glorious color. Have you ever tried to count how many shades of green there are in a forest? Or how many shades of red in a bouquet of roses?

Why did God bother with all those colors? The answer is simple, and yet difficult to comprehend: because He loves us so much. God's love for us is so deep, so high, so wide, so vast, our finite minds can't grasp it. Everything He does, He does out of love for us. Even create color.

Lord, thank You for this beautifully colorful world You've created. Open my eyes to see all the many colors of You. Amen.

Be Careful to Love

So be very careful to love the LORD your God.

Joshua 23:11

"Be careful!" you tell your preschooler as he climbs the monkey bars.

"Be careful!" your mom says as you set off on a road trip.

We're so used to the phrase *be careful* (meaning *watch out!*) that today's verse might not make sense. But here, Joshua was stressing that the Israelites needed to *pay close attention* to their relationship with God. They needed to stop being careless.

We, too, should be thoughtful about our relationship with Jesus. If we're honest, most of us would admit that we're easily distracted by the worries of everyday life. And if we're not careful (there's that word again!), we'll wake up one day and wonder, *What happened? Why does God feel so far away?*

Nothing is as important as "lov[ing] the LORD your God." If you've been careless about your spiritual life, determine to pay closer attention and to do whatever it takes to invite Jesus into your every day.

Lord, please forgive me if I've been careless instead of careful about our relationship. Teach me to always pay attention to my love for You. Amen.

One Body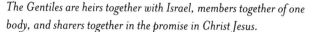

The Gentiles are heirs together with Israel, members together of one body, and sharers together in the promise in Christ Jesus.

Ephesians 3:6

Racial prejudice and conflict are nothing new. Because of sin, people have found (or invented) reasons to hate each other since the fall of Adam. God, however, has a very different viewpoint of the differences in people. In Acts 10:34–35, Peter said, "I now realize how true it is that God does not show favoritism but accepts from every nation the one who fears him and does what is right."

God's love is perfect, and He loves every human being in the same way. Shouldn't we, then, also love *all* people? We who are believers are "members together of one body." Should the leg hate the arm? Or the eye hate the ear? How can a body function if its parts hate each other?

God's command to love one another doesn't say, "if you're of the same race" or "if you live on the same side of the tracks." It simply says . . . love one another.

Thank You, Lord, that You love all people, regardless of what we look like or where we come from. Help me to love as You do. Amen.

Your New Name

"To the one who is victorious, I will give . . . that person a white stone with a new name written on it, known only to the one who receives it."

Revelation 2:17

Why did God sometimes give people new names, as He did for Abram, Sarai, and Simon? For some, a new name might denote the passing of an old identity and emergence of a new one (Hosea 2:1). For Jacob, his name change to "Israel" was to signify his destiny as the father of that nation. Jesus nicknamed James and John the "Sons of Thunder"—a term of endearment that also described their personalities. A change of name can also symbolize that a person has become a new creation by his or her faith in Christ (2 Corinthians 5:17).

Have you ever thought to ask the Lord for a new name? Maybe you're stepping into an exciting new season, or God has recently made your destiny clear to you, or you're stepping more fully into your true identity. Maybe you've recently fallen in love with Jesus all over again, and you suspect that He has a term of endearment for you. Just ask Him. You might be surprised at His answer.

Lord, I know You love me, but exactly how do You see me? What do You call me? Have You given me a new name? Please speak to my heart. Amen.

God's SOS

Have mercy on me, O God, according to your unfailing love. . . .
Create in me a pure heart, O God, and renew a steadfast spirit
within me.

Psalm 51:1, 10

If you've ever had to clean burnt food from a pan, you know what a strenuous job that can be. You scrub and scrub, but there are always a few persistent bits that cling to the bottom of the pan. No effort of yours is adequate for the job, and you finally give up.

God has His own brand of cleanser, and it's always effective. If we've sinned—no matter how gravely or for how long—and we repent of those sins, God will cleanse us, until our hearts are absolutely clean and pure, whiter than snow, with no stubborn spots remaining. No effort of ours will do it; only God can make us clean again.

King David knew the power of God's cleansing. He wrote today's psalm after he'd committed both adultery and murder. But He trusted in the power of God's cleansing and in His unfailing love. You can too.

Lord, thank You for always being willing to make my heart clean
again. Use Your cleansing power on me! Amen.

God's Children

To those who believed in his name, he gave the right to become children of God.

John 1:12

The ideal family, which includes two functional, mentally healthy adults, is no longer as common as it used to be. Tragically, lots of families suffer from an absent or abusive parent. Children endure abandonment and neglect and are often forced to grow up too quickly. Years later, those same children are still wandering through life, wondering who they are and to whom they belong because they lacked the love they needed to flourish as adults.

Thankfully, we can discover where we belong (and to whom we belong) because it's all written in the Bible. As John 1:12–13 says, we are children of God. And we can be healed of childhood trauma as the perfect love of God binds up our wounds, little by little, until we're whole again.

We have a place in the family of God. God is waiting for His children to join Him—we need only accept Him.

I'm Your child, Lord. I know right where I belong—in Your family, as Your beloved son/daughter. Amen.

Love and Duty

"When you've done everything I'm telling you to do, just say, 'We're servants, unworthy of extra consideration or thanks; we're just doing our duty.'"

Luke 17:10 THE VOICE

You've opened your home for a women's Bible study every Thursday night, and you feel good about being able to share God's love in this way. But then, during the first class, someone mentions that she's part of a prison ministry. Someone else spends every summer building schools in a Third World country. And someone else has just published a book about discipleship. How can you compete?

You can't . . . and *you shouldn't*. Everyone has opportunities to love their neighbors and serve the kingdom of God, but in different ways. Your way is specific to your unique abilities and gifts, and it's tailored for this season in your life. As long as you're happily following God's lead to the best of your ability, don't worry about what everyone else is doing. Your method of service is cause for neither shame *nor* pride. As Luke observed, you're "just doing [your] duty" to the God who loves and leads you.

Lord, I surrender the need to compete with my brothers and sisters, who love You as I do! Amen.

MAY

....

From everlasting to everlasting the LORD's
love is with those who fear him.

Psalm 103:17

Giving Strangers the Benefit of the Doubt

Love bears all things, believes all things.

1 Corinthians 13:7 ESV

You're creeping down the road at twenty-five miles per hour. The speed limit is forty. One especially irritated driver blows his horn and shouts as he passes you by. You feel guilty and foolish. If only he knew you were running a fever and just trying to make it the last mile home.

What if, for one day, you assume that anyone who irritates you is having a worse day than you? Instead of attributing selfish motives to them, give them the benefit of the doubt. That restaurant server who forgets to bring you ketchup? What if she's covering the job of two employees at once?

Every time someone annoys you, tell yourself: "His intentions are good." "She's doing her best." "He deserves some extra grace today." It's an easy way to love your neighbor. And at the end of the day, chances are you'll be much happier and at peace—and so will those around you.

Forgive me, Lord, for always assuming the worst about the people who annoy me. Help me to give others the benefit of the doubt. Amen.

Giving Family the Benefit of the Doubt

The LORD is slow to anger, abounding in love.

Numbers 14:18

How about taking yesterday's experiment one step further? Spend the whole day giving the benefit of the doubt to your family. This might actually be more difficult to do!

When you're about to criticize a family member for something he's done or she's said, remember author Shannon Alder's words: "Critics judge things based on what is outside of their content of understanding."[1] That simply means we tend to assume the worst because we don't know all the facts.

We like to think we know our loved ones inside and out, but we can't possibly know everything in a person's heart, or all the thoughts that vex that person. When your dad is being especially grumpy, he might be anxious over a bill you know nothing about. When your brother cuts you off in mid-sentence for the fifth time, he might be overwhelmed by an overloaded schedule.

"The LORD is slow to anger, abounding in love." May He help us to be the same.

Lord, I want to offer my family the same patience and understanding I give to strangers. Help me offer the people in my life the benefit of the doubt. Amen.

If You Love Me

"If you love Me, you will keep My commands."

John 14:15 HCSB

"If you love me, then you'll . . ."

For millennia, human beings have been attempting to coerce their loved ones into action by using this phrase. But "if . . . then" ultimatums don't work well in marriage—or any other relationship, for that matter. Granted, where there's love, there should also be certain behaviors; for example, a man who loves his wife should be faithful. But we tend to use the "If you love me . . ." phrase to strong-arm one another into behaving a certain way. That's called manipulation, and it damages relationships.

Ultimately, only our Lord has the right to say, "If you love Me . . ." And He *did* say it, as recorded in John 14:15. He defined what our love for Him would require—and then He went to the cross and fulfilled those requirements for us, so that when we fail, we'll be forgiven. Now, *that's* love.

Show me, Lord, if I've been manipulating any of my loved ones
instead of loving them the way You've called me to love them. Amen.

If God Loves Me

I pray that you . . . grasp how wide and long and high and deep is the love of Christ.

f you love me . . ." If it's wrong to use that phrase on others, it's infinitely more wrong to use it on God. But don't we sometimes do exactly that? *God, if You love me, You'll fix my finances . . . fix my marriage . . . allow me to get pregnant.*

Sometimes we assume that if God loves us, He'll answer our prayers with a yes—as quickly as possible. But we have no business stipulating what God will and won't do. He doesn't have to prove Himself. He's already demonstrated His love by sending Jesus.

God knows what we do not, and His love reflects that. For example, we might be assuming God will give us a promotion if He loves us, when He's actually planning to move us into a new, better job! God's love for us is infinite and unchanging— whether or not He's giving us what we think we want.

You offer me the purest, deepest love that's ever existed, Lord, and I refuse to put my own expectations on it. Amen.

Blame Versus Empathy

Mourn with those who mourn.

Person 1: Did you hear about the girl who was nearly
  kidnapped from the grocery store?
Person 2: Where was her mother?
Person 1: Just a few feet away. She got distracted for a
  split second . . .
Person 2: What's *wrong* with her? I'd never give a predator
  a chance to grab my child!

We see it all the time on social media: something happens
to a child, and long before the details come to light, the
parents are lambasted for negligence. Why do people attack
each other like this? Because of fear. We want to think we're
immune to such suffering. The moment we point the finger of
blame at the person who's suffering, we can say, *That would never
happen to me*, which makes us feel safe. But then we've cut ourselves off from those who suffer. To offer love and comfort to
others, we must be willing to say, "That could have been me."

*Lord, help me never to see myself as above suffering. Help me not to
blame others for their tragedies, but to reach out in love. Amen.*

The God Who "Gets" You

Whoever loves God is known by God.

1 Corinthians 8:3

Think of a time someone gave you a small, silly gift that meant something very personal, something only you and the giver understood. Or maybe there was a time you laughed out loud because a friend texted you a funny meme that perfectly represented a certain aspect of your personality. Gestures like these cost so little, yet they can mean so much, quickly bringing a smile to our faces. The fact that they're very personal and specific lets us know that the giver "gets" us.

We all long to have people in our lives who really "get" us—who know our hopes and dreams, our quirks and personalities—and celebrate them. But no one "gets" us better than God. He knows us inside and out, upside down and backward. Maybe you're a night owl, or you crave anchovies, or you love to draw cartoons. These details matter to God. Isn't it reassuring to know that He "gets" you?

Lord, I love that You love me in such a very personal way. You know all my quirks and flaws—and You cherish me anyway. Amen.

Tempered and Tough

We know that suffering produces perseverance; perseverance,
character; and character, hope.

Romans 5:3–4

*T*empering is a process that improves the toughness and elasticity of iron-based alloys, such as steel, through heating and cooling. The resulting material is tougher, less brittle, and more stable than before. The ultimate goal of tempering is to yield the best-quality material possible.

Have you wondered why it seems God is allowing one fiery trial after another into your life? Are you feeling overwhelmed, wishing He'd give you a break? He might well be tempering you. It may seem harsh, but it's because He loves you. You see, God has a job for you, and He wants you to be durable enough to handle it. Tempering makes you more stable in your beliefs and principles. You'll be less brittle and more elastic, more willing to adapt and to change. Tempering shapes you into who God created you to be.

Every Christian needs tempering according to his or her unique personality, strengths, weaknesses, life experiences, and God-given tasks. If you're in the fire, thank God for finding you worthy of the process.

Thank You, Lord, for taking me through the process of tempering.
I choose to hang on tight and trust You to make me far better for it.
Amen.

Your Spiritual Love Language

I will sing to the LORD because he is good to me.

Psalm 13:6 NLT

Countless couples have strengthened their relationships through the wildly popular book *The 5 Love Languages* by Gary Chapman. This book explains that all people communicate love in a specific way, such as through quality time, words of affirmation, or physical touch.[2] What might happen if we applied the concepts in this book to our relationship with God as well?

For example, you might feel closest to God during your morning Bible study. If so, Bible study might be your main love language. Do you love communicating with God through songs that you write? Then spend some time each day as the Lord's psalmist. Meanwhile, your best friend's spiritual love language might involve corporate prayer, and your teenager's might consist of playing a guitar or keyboard.

Be careful not to compare your spiritual love language with anyone else's. There's no wrong way to spend time with God! The important thing is to find out what your language is, and become fluent in it.

Help me discover my spiritual love language, Father. And then teach me to speak it fluently. Amen.

Loving God's Authority

*Who has wrapped up the waters in a cloak? . . . What is his name,
and what is the name of his son? Surely you know!*

Proverbs 30:4

Ocean tides are fascinating. In Canada's Bay of Fundy, the difference between the high and low tides can be as high as a whopping fifty-six feet! Many factors account for ocean tides: gravity, the sun, the earth's rotation, and the moon . . . but the ultimate reason for the tides is that God decided they should be so, and nature submits to the laws established by God. Coastlines all over the world have been cresting twice each day since creation, without fail, simply because God is in authority.

Do you desire to demonstrate your love for God? Then submit every single part of who you are to His authority, just as the ocean does. Obedience is often uncomfortable and inconvenient, but it's a vital way to actively show your love. Say yes when God prompts you to do something. Hold nothing back. Be as steady and compliant as the tides.

Your authority trumps everything, Lord! May I be as steady as the tides, always ready to obey You without resistance. Amen.

Practical Love

The word of the LORD came to Elijah: ". . . Hide in the Kerith Ravine. . . . I have directed the ravens to supply you with food."
1 Kings 17:2–4

It happened so fast: one minute, the young woman's life was normal, and the next, her husband was in the hospital with a badly broken leg. Her head was spinning; she had a thousand things to do, phone calls to make, insurance papers to file . . .

Just then an older woman from church walked into the hospital room. After a quick hug, she asked, "What do you need *right this minute*?" The young wife hesitated, then pulled out a small package. "I have to mail this by four o'clock! I was on my way to the post office when I got the call . . ."

The older woman took the package and said, "I'll be back soon." The young woman's relief was immense. Suddenly she knew everything was going to be okay.

Sometimes, love is expressed in grand ways. But sometimes, love is practical. A mailed package. A changed tire. A meal delivered in a ravine by a raven.

Teach me, Lord, to express love in practical ways, especially to those who are feeling overwhelmed. Amen.

He Is Faithful

If we are unfaithful, He remains faithful, for He is not able to deny Himself.

2 Timothy 2:13 THE VOICE

There's a man with autism who's been a clerk at a government installation for more than thirty years. Both administrators and coworkers have only praise for him because he's completely dependable, having missed work only a few times, and then only due to serious illness. He faithfully fulfills every responsibility—never shirking his duties, wasting time, or doing his work with anything less than excellence. He's truly a faithful worker.

God is our perfect example of faithfulness. Even when we shirk our duties, waste time, or do our work with less than excellence, He remains faithful. He never breaks a promise. He never changes. He is not fickle or capricious. God is never lazy, never wastes time, and never does His work with less than perfection. His Word is absolute truth, and we can completely depend on it. Why is God so faithful to us? Because He said He would be.

Lord, in a world that's so unstable and undependable, it's so reassuring to know I can always depend on You. Thank You! Amen.

Love and Technology

I hope to see you soon, and we will talk face to face.

3 John 1:14

Dinner at 6? Applebee's. My treat.

Send a text like that to your best friend, and it'll probably put a smile on his face. But send it to the young woman who just joined your home church group, and you probably won't ever get a first date. Why? Because technology is a great tool under the right conditions, and a scourge under the wrong ones.

In 2006, the *New York Times* ran a story about a certain retail store chain that laid off four hundred employees via e-mail.[3] No wonder someone called the method "dehumanizing," as it implied that the higher-ups didn't think their staff was worth a personal meeting.

Texting, e-mail, and other forms of messaging are convenient and valuable—except when they're not. The next time you're about to hit "Send" and you feel a little check in your spirit, listen to it. Make sure the occasion doesn't call for a more loving approach, like a face-to-face conversation.

Thank You so much, Lord, for the gift of technology, but help me be a good steward of it by always showing others the love and respect they deserve. Amen.

When You Don't Understand

"Can a mother forget the baby at her breast and have no compassion on the child she has borne? . . . I will not forget you!"

A newborn doesn't question her mother's embrace; she simply receives it. A toddler has no idea why Daddy straps him into a car seat or takes his hand as they cross the street.

We can't wrap our minds around the ways of God any more than a little child can comprehend the love of his mother and father. But just like a child, for us understanding love is not a prerequisite to receiving it. And like a child who thrives under the care of his parents, we can flourish and grow even when God's ways are mysterious.

The Holy Spirit teaches us and reveal truths about God, but there are certain times when circumstances don't make sense and we just have to trust Him. Sometimes we have to be okay with the fact that understanding will come later. In the meantime, we can rest in His ability and love, and thrive under His care.

I trust You, Lord, even though there's no way I can fully understand Your great big love and Your mysterious ways. Amen.

Finishing Well

Gideon made the gold into an ephod. . . . All Israel prostituted themselves by worshiping it there, and it became a snare to Gideon and his family.

Judges 8:27

$\mathcal{J}$f you've been a Christian for any length of time, you're probably familiar with the story of Gideon, who fought and won a battle against more than a hundred thousand soldiers with only three hundred men. But what most people don't realize is that after this astounding feat, Gideon requested enough gold from the plunder to make an ephod (priestly vest), which the Israelites then worshiped as an idol—and which "became a snare" even to Gideon! After valiantly proving his devotion to God, Gideon stumbled into idolatry.

If you've never heard this part of Gideon's story, you're not alone. Often, we skip the details that contradict the happily ever after we long for. But there's a vital lesson here: Many people start badly but then finish well. Others start well, but finish badly.

In the Christian journey, we must be single-minded about our love for God. When life is difficult and temptations are all around you, focus on the goal—and finish well.

Lord, I love You now, and I'm determined to love You even more when I come to the end of the journey. Help me to finish well. Amen.

Where He Is

"I have compassion on the crowd, because they have been with me now three days and have nothing to eat. . . . And some of them have come from far away."

Mark 8:2–3 ESV

Choose Vacation #1 or #2:

- Vacation #1 is a camping trip involving ticks, a thunderstorm, and meals made with rehydrated eggs— spent with someone you love who adores you in return.
- Vacation #2 involves a 5-star hotel, gorgeous weather, a personal chef, and a swimming pool. But you must spend the whole time with someone who'd rather have a root canal than be in your company.

If you're like most people, you picked the camping trip because even a difficult experience can be redeemed when spent with someone who loves you so much that he or she is happy just to be where you are.

In Mark 8, Jesus had compassion on the people who'd traveled a long way—just because they wanted to be where He was. God delights in that kind of devotion. It moves Him when we're less concerned with our own comfort than we are with being in His presence simply because we love Him.

As long as I can be where You are, Lord, I'll be satisfied. Your love is what I need more than anything else. Amen.

24/7

I will praise the LORD, who counsels me; even at night my heart instructs me.

Psalm 16:7

You fall asleep on the couch by nine o'clock at night, but the moment you stumble to bed and pull the blanket up to your chin, you're wide awake, your mind buzzing with anxious thoughts. The pillow feels lumpy, and your internal temperature swings from too hot to too cold. Groaning in frustration, you resign yourself to another sleepless night. If this sounds familiar, you're not alone: according to the Sleep Health Foundation, one in three people has trouble sleeping.[4] But there's hope: God is available 24/7 to comfort us. In fact, Psalm 16 tells us He'll counsel and speak to our hearts in the night hours.

God loves and cares for you every moment of every day. He's completely in control whether you're awake or asleep. So you can rest easy and sleep when you're meant to sleep. Even if your eyes do pop open at two in the morning, He's still on the job, watching over you.

Lord, remind me when I struggle in the middle of the night that You love me and You're with Me every moment, day or night. Amen.

Like You've Never Been Hurt

He heals the brokenhearted and binds up their wounds.

Psalm 147:3

ost of us have heard the saying, "Dance like there's nobody watching, and love like you've never been hurt." The point of the second half of this saying is that sometimes, love leads to pain, which can then prevent us from making the "mistake" of loving again. When we love someone, we do take a risk. We put ourselves out there. We bare our hearts, which leaves us vulnerable to being hurt.

Maybe you've been wounded, and the idea of forgiving the person who hurt you seems foolish or even impossible. It's true that some relationships are toxic, and we need to distance ourselves, but most are worth our time, sacrifice, and forgiveness. God is willing and able to heal you of those past offenses, which will then free you to love like you've never been hurt once again. Let God pour His love into you; then you'll be able to offer it to others—even when it's risky.

Help me, Lord, to forgive those who've hurt me so I can love others generously, just as You love me. Amen.

Unlimited Love

Your love, LORD, reaches to the heavens, your faithfulness to the skies.

Psalm 36:5

When dark clouds, thunder, and lightning approach, we know it's going to rain. A young woman clutches her swollen abdomen, and we know a baby is coming. Lovely daffodils lift their golden heads to the sky, nodding in the breeze, and we know spring will soon arrive. We know many things, but because we humans are not all-knowing, our knowledge is limited. That's why God gave us these faithful harbingers to warn us about or to announce coming events. In His great love, God wants to prepare for what is to come.

And what is ultimately to come is the great Day of Judgment. But God does not leave us unprepared. Not only did He warn us that the Day is coming; He also sent His Son to provide what we need—a way to be forgiven for all we've done wrong. Why? Because, as David proclaimed in Psalm 36, God's love for us "reaches to the heavens."

Father, You've blessed me by truly and deeply loving me—so much that You sent Your own Son to save me. Thank You. Amen.

Loving Your Church Family

Love each other as brothers and sisters. Be tenderhearted, and keep a humble attitude.

1 Peter 3:8 NLT

It's 7 a.m. on Sunday: time to get ready for church. You should be looking forward to the day, but instead you're struggling with guilt because, frankly, you'd rather sit on the porch and eat bagels all morning. When did you start to dread getting together with your church community? Your lack of loving feelings for your brothers and sisters has you in a tailspin.

If you were to describe your church family, would you naturally use the word *love*, as Peter did? If the answer is no, you might want to figure out why. Maybe there's a valid reason for your negative feelings and you need some counsel. Or maybe you need to work through a past offense. Either way, talk to the Lord about it. He'll show you where the problem lies, and He'll deepen your love for your church family as you ask Him to enlarge your heart.

Lord, help me to love my church family with all my heart. If I need to be more patient or forgiving, please make a change in me. Amen.

The God Who Sees

When the LORD saw that Leah was not loved, he enabled her to conceive.

Genesis 29:31

Are you among the countless movie fans who've watched *Sleepless in Seattle* or *You've Got Mail* a dozen times? A key reason that these romantic comedies are classics after all these years is because we know that, before the credits roll, love will win the day. Tom Hanks's character will finally (and adorably) exchange a kiss with Meg Ryan's character, and everyone will live happily ever after.

But real life doesn't always look like that. Sometimes, real life stinks. It involves sorrow and tears and rejection. Maybe you feel the way Leah did: unloved and undervalued. Maybe you've loved someone who rejected you. You can take comfort in the fact that God *sees*, just as He saw Leah. And He cares about your story. Your pain is His pain, and the details of your life matter more to Him than you could ever imagine.

You're not alone. God sees you, and in the end, love does win the day.

Lord, thank You for being a God who sees everything I experience, and who loves and cares for me through every joyful and every painful moment. Amen.

Learning from Others

Plans fail for lack of counsel, but with many advisers they succeed.

Have you ever met someone who insisted that Christians shouldn't read any book except the Bible? The rationale is that only God's Word contains pure truth, and therefore, we shouldn't seek counsel from anywhere else. While it's true that the Bible consists of 100 percent truth, that doesn't mean we can't benefit from others' thoughts on the Bible. Otherwise, because we're *all* flawed, we'd have no business ever discussing God with one another, or offering advice, or examining doctrine together.

We can learn a lot from other people who love and serve God, or who loved and served Him when they were alive. Some might know Him more intimately than we do, and others—because each of our lives is made up of unique circumstances—simply know Him in a *different* way. Don't hesitate to share with others what you've discovered about the love of God, or to learn from their own journeys.

Thank You, Father, for my brothers and sisters in Christ. May I learn from them and speak into their lives, as well. Amen.

Simply Patient

Love is patient.

1 Corinthians 13:4

*L*ove is patient. This phrase is so simple that it seems as if something must be missing. But as with many of the most beautiful things in life, we try to make it more complicated than it is. When one of God's instructions starts to feel complex and confusing, stop and read it again at face value, in its simplest form: *Love is patient.* End of story.

Yes, sometimes love means making a big sacrifice or splurging on an expensive date night with your sweetheart. But for today it might mean allowing your toddler to spend eight minutes doing what you could do in thirty seconds just so he can feel the joy of accomplishment. It might mean listening to your coworker talk about the novel she's writing even though you'd rather spend your time in the breakroom, lost in your own thoughts.

Sometimes, the most loving thing we can do is simply be patient.

Lord, don't let me overlook opportunities to show love in the simplest of ways. Amen.

Sing a Song

Let all who take refuge in you be glad; let them ever sing for joy. . . .
Those who love your name may rejoice in you.

Psalm 5:11

f you've ever gone camping or slept with your windows open, you know that birds begin singing very early in the morning—and many don't stop until the last bit of daylight has disappeared. Some birds sing more than two thousand times each day! Apparently songbirds don't run out of things to sing about. And neither should we. The psalmist told us that those who take refuge in the Lord and love His name have reason to rejoice in song. The good news is that you don't need to have a pitch-perfect voice to do so.

Make a habit of singing to the Lord as you commute to work, fill your car with gas, or scramble eggs. Sing songs that express your love for God or acknowledge His love for you. You might not rack up two thousand songs a day, but you *will* discover that singing even the simplest tunes increases your love for the One who hears you.

Lord, teach me to sing with joy and with love for You in my heart.
Amen.

The Gift of Silence

They sat on the ground with [Job] for seven days and seven nights. No one said a word to him, because they saw how great his suffering was.

Job 2:13

There are a million ways to express love and concern when someone is hurting. We can lend a listening ear, send a card, or offer to pray with him or her. But sometimes the most loving thing we can offer, especially when someone's pain is extreme, is silence. When Job lost everything that was near and dear to him, his three friends came to see him. Once they opened their mouths, they said some very unwise things. But in the beginning—for seven days and nights—they simply sat with their devastated friend.

Sometimes, a person in pain needs our quiet presence far more than our frenzied words of advice. (The effort to keep our mouths closed can actually require a lot more sacrifice than making a casserole or ordering flowers!) The next time a friend is faced with a crisis, ask yourself, *What does he really need from me? Am I willing to take the time to sit quietly with him?*

Lord, make me sensitive to what people need most. Help me be willing to show love to a friend who's hurting by simply being present. Amen.

The Gift of Honor

Give to everyone what you owe them: . . . If respect, then respect; if honor, then honor.

Romans 13:7

The media has done great damage to the concept of honor in the past few decades. It's not unusual to see the members of a TV family belittle each other as a studio audience laughs. The more sarcastic the remarks, the more we're entertained. Television has so warped our ideas about love, decency, and honor that, if we're not careful, we'll absorb the wrong mindsets, which will then show up in the way we treat others. We'll buy into the idea that it's perfectly okay to ridicule someone when he or she doesn't measure up to our expectations. But this isn't what the Bible teaches.

God tells us to honor one another, even those who are difficult to love. To honor someone is to treat him or her with respect. This won't always come easily, but it'll always be the right thing to do.

Lord, help me take an honest look at how I treat others. May I honor them at all times and in all ways. Amen.

All Things

In all things God works for the good of those who love him.

You blew it.

Maybe you said something completely out of character—just as your boss walked into the room. Or you made a risky investment—and lost thousands. Or you overreacted—and now your teenager is in tears.

You love the Lord and want to please Him, but you're convinced that nothing good will ever come from this mess you've made.

King David could relate. He loved God with all his heart, yet he managed to make some huge mistakes. Still, all was not lost. For example, plenty of sorrow came when he sinned against God with Bathsheba, yet that marriage later produced Solomon. God used Solomon to change history and even write portions of the Old Testament. He was living proof that not only does God correct us when we sin, but He also exchanges our wreckage for His blessings. God works not *some* things for good but "all things . . . for the good of those who love him"—including you.

Thank You, Lord, for using even my worst mistakes for my greater good. You truly are a great God. Amen.

Wondrous Love

"Greater love has no one than this: to lay down one's life for one's friends."

John 15:13

Jesus faced many trials during His time on earth. But have you ever considered this: He *willingly* left the glories of a perfect heaven to come and live for thirty-three years on a sin-riddled earth. He left a place where He was continuously praised and glorified to live in a place where He was mocked, rejected, and even hated. He went from a place of no pain and no suffering to earth, where he would experience unimaginable torture; from a place where there's no discomfort to live here with us and experience hunger, thirst, cold, heat, loneliness, frustration, and exhaustion; and from a place of pure love to a world filled with jealousy, deception, lies, immorality, and cheating.

We, and this world, had nothing to offer Jesus but darkness, sin, and suffering, yet He came for us anyway. And when He did, He gave us *all* of Himself—all His compassion, forgiveness, love, and truth. What wondrous love!

Father God, how can I possibly thank You for Your wondrous love?
You said we can praise You through obedience, so help me to obey.
Amen.

Love Versus Aggression

Those who are still under the control of their sinful nature can never please God.

Romans 8:8 NLT

When it comes to communication, are you quiet and compliant? Or do you tend to speak your mind quickly and forcefully? Our society values confidence, but there's a fine line between *bold* communication and *aggressive* communication.

Aggression isn't always obvious, and bullies aren't always big and brawny. Granted, sometimes an aggressive person might raise his voice, become angry, or use some other in-your-face tactic. But aggression can also be subtle, such as interrupting instead of listening, being sarcastic or snarky, giving little thought to people's feelings before spouting an opinion, teasing in a way that's not funny, humiliating others, or stooping to emotional blackmail.

If you see yourself in these examples, take heart; you can learn to communicate in more loving ways. All it takes is humility, the desire to become more Christlike, and some divine help from God.

Is there someone with whom I've been aggressive and unloving, Lord? Help me to communicate with compassion and love instead. Amen.

Love and Passivity

For the Spirit God gave us does not make us timid, but gives us power, love and self-discipline.

2 Timothy 1:7

Many people tend to be more passive when communicating. That is, they might be more hesitant to speak, more willing to let others do the talking. This doesn't necessarily present relationship problems, unless you are *excessively* passive, so reluctant to speak your mind that others are left scrambling, trying to figure out what you're thinking and feeling. You might agree too quickly, saying yes to every suggestion while secretly answering no. You might even shut down only to complain about a situation later. Because feelings of powerlessness go along with passivity, you might even catch yourself slamming a frying pan onto a burner rather than expressing unhappiness or anger in a healthy way.

Does this description hit close to home? If so, you can learn to be more assertive and less passive. Realize that passivity is based in fear, but Christians are called to courage. Ask the Lord to teach you to express your feelings in a loving but authentic way.

Am I overly passive, Lord? If so, please show me, and give me the courage to speak in loving and truthful ways. Amen.

Passive-Aggression

The speech of the honest keeps them free.

Proverbs 12:6 THE VOICE

One of the most damaging methods of communication is passive-aggression. In fact, it's hardly worthy of being called *communication*. It's manipulation, and it *never* demonstrates love.

How does it work? Imagine a woman is about to leave a store with her eight-year-old son, but he doesn't want to go. He knows better than to throw a full-blown tantrum, so he sits on the floor and goes limp. "Stop it, Tommy!" scolds Mom. "I'm not doing anything," he answers.

Technically, he's *not* doing anything—except making it impossible for Mom to leave. Sometimes adults act like Tommy: A supervisor gives an employee a to-do list; she resents the implication that she has more time than he does, but rather than be honest, she "forgets" the list until finally, in frustration, he delegates it to someone else.

Sometimes the passive-aggressive route seems like the easiest solution, but love is honest, not manipulative. And we owe it to others—and to God—to be honest.

Lord, if I've been passive-aggressive with the people around me, help me to talk to them in a mature way that's pleasing to You. Amen.

Assertive Love

"All you need to say is simply 'Yes' or 'No'; anything beyond this comes from the evil one."

Matthew 5:37

Assertiveness: the perfect middle of the road between passivity and aggression. Assertiveness is the loving, sensible way to communicate in countless situations.

The assertive person is expressive while also being thoughtful. If you and a friend who's naturally assertive decide to go out to eat, she'll neither demand her way—"I hope you're okay with Chinese because that's what we're having"—nor will she coyly refuse to express an opinion. Assertiveness never shouts, "Give me my rights!" (That's aggression.) But it also never says, "Feel free to stomp on my rights." (That's passivity.) Instead, it protects the rights of *both* parties.

We know that assertiveness and love can go hand in hand because Jesus often exhibited both. Do you wish you were more assertive? Then practice being candid but not confrontational. Be willing to talk through conflicts rather than letting your emotions take over. And always respect the other person's boundaries while also honoring your own.

Lord, when You were here on earth, You were both compassionate and firm. Help me to follow Your example. Amen.

JUNE

How precious are your thoughts about me,
O God. They cannot be numbered!

Psalm 139:17 NLT

Destination: Unknown

The LORD had said to Abram, "Go from your country, your people and your father's household to the land I will show you."

magine being told by someone you can't see to pack up everything you own, take your spouse and kids, and go. Destination? Unknown. You have no idea where you're going or how long you'll be gone: A week? A month? A lifetime? Will you ever see your friends and neighbors again? What will you encounter on the journey? All you know for certain is that it's God Himself who's told you to go, and it's God who's promised to show you the way. Would you go?

Abram did. He knew that the God who loved him would not abandon him. He knew—and completely trusted—God's faithfulness. So he packed up everything, and he went, ready to follow the Lord wherever the Lord led him. His destination was unknown, but his Leader was well-known and trusted.

Do you believe in God's love and faithfulness enough to be willing to follow Him to a destination unknown?

Lord, help me to trust You enough to say, "I'll go wherever, whenever—and I'll do whatever You ask of me." Amen.

The Common Man

We are the clay, you are the potter; we are all the work of your hand.

Isaiah 64:8

Moses, Abraham, Joshua, Peter, Paul, Billy Graham, Rev. Martin Luther King Jr., Mother Teresa—all were just common men and women, but in the hands of our miracle-working Lord, they became people of valor who did uncommonly great things for God. In the eyes of the God who created us, we're all valuable. Like the potter who makes a stunning vase from a lump of clay, He can transform each of us into beautiful, worthwhile, and productive instruments for His use—if we allow Him to.

Because God created us, we belong more completely to Him than we do to ourselves! Often, however, we choose to cling to our independence and refuse to let Him mold us into who He wants us to be. But God is much wiser than we are! Give yourself completely to Him; then watch what He'll do in, for, and through you. He's the Master Potter, and He'll make something remarkable of you.

Lord, take me and use me. Transform me into the person that You, in Your incomparable wisdom, want me to be. Amen.

Lovely Thoughts

Whatever is true, whatever is noble, whatever is right, whatever is pure, whatever is lovely, whatever is admirable—if anything is excellent or praiseworthy—think about such things.

Philippians 4:8

In 2 Corinthians 10:5, the Bible tells us to take every one of our thoughts captive. This can be a difficult task, because society tells us that we can't help what we think. However, Philippians 4:8 says we can, indeed, make a deliberate effort to *choose* what we think about. The verse then goes on to list what sort of thoughts we should choose. Imagine if we consistently focused our thoughts on things that were true, noble, right, pure, lovely, admirable, excellent, and praiseworthy. It would be virtually impossible to feel blue, anxious, worried—or tempted! What a love-centered life we would live!

God never tells us to do anything that's impossible for us to do (with His help). Consequently, when He tells us to take our thoughts captive, He means we should do just that. A pure thought life leads to a pure heart. And a pure heart leads to a life of love.

Lord, I want to be obedient to You. Help me take my thoughts captive and think only about those things that are pleasing to You. Amen.

Through the Storms

Even though I walk through the darkest valley, I will fear no evil.

Psalm 23:4

It had been a terrible thunderstorm. The tempest seemed to have parked directly over the apartment complex, and there it howled, grumbled, rumbled, and flashed for about two hours. In the morning, the residents went to their windows, expecting a mess of tree limbs and pieces of roofing in the parking lot. To their amazement, the lot was clear. In His love, God had brought them all safely through yet another storm.

Even though the storms of life can be threatening and frightening, if we love and trust God, He will see us through. He might not stop the storms from coming, but He *will* take us by the hand and lead us through them—if we let Him. After all, He has said He'll never leave us or forsake us (Deuteronomy 31:6), and God always keeps His promises. Will you trust Him with your troubles and difficulties—the storms of *your* life? He'll see you safely through.

God, You're my heavenly Father, and You promise to take care of me. Please help me trust You through the storms. Amen.

Stand Firm

Stand firm and see the deliverance the LORD will give you. . . . Do not be afraid; do not be discouraged.

2 Chronicles 20:17

Behold the lowly dandelion! According to the Maine Organic Farmers and Gardeners Association, dandelion roots can grow fifteen feet into the ground. These little weeds are masters of survival and practically impossible to get rid of. "A one-inch bit of dandelion root can grow a whole new dandelion," and "dandelion leaves can shove their way through gravel and cement."[1] Dandelions stand firm and are victorious in their own small way.

In today's verse, Jahaziel reminded the Hebrews, who were facing a vast enemy army, that God would give them victory—*if* they stood firm and trusted Him. "For the battle is not yours, but God's," he told them (2 Chronicles 20:15). In like manner, when we're faced with the enemy, Satan, we must remember that God is greater and mightier than *any* army. We can trust Him and His love for us, knowing that, if we stand firm in our faith, we *will* be victorious.

Lord, how marvelous it is to know You're mightier than any enemy we face. Thank You for fighting my battles for me! Amen.

Child of God

See what great love the Father has lavished on us, that we should be called children of God!

1 John 3:1

Not too long ago, social media went wild over a video of a young adult who asked her foster mother to adopt her and handed her adoption papers. She loved her foster mom and wanted to be her "real" child, despite the fact that she herself was already old enough to be a mother.[2]

We all want—and need—to belong. This need goes even deeper than the need for a human parent, however, and is even more spiritual than physical. This need has rightly been dubbed "a God-shaped hole," an accurate description because only God Himself can fill it. What's truly amazing is that God loves us so much *He* wants *us* to be His children! God already has everything He needs, yet He wants to adopt us for Himself.

When we're reborn into the kingdom of God, He "signs our adoption papers." From that moment on, we're His children—and He is our Father—forever.

I love You, Lord, and I thank You for adopting me as Your child. Amen.

Better with Time

I love those who love me, and those who seek me find me.

Proverbs 8:17

Spaghetti. Chili. Soup. Lasagna. Most would agree that these dishes are better the second day, after they've sat for a while on the stove and then in the fridge. Why is this? Because some things are just better with time. The flavors develop, and the spices have a chance to infuse into the whole dish.

Revelation talks of a "first love" (2:4), and some would say that early, passionate love diminishes quickly, but it doesn't have to. Love that's built on the right foundation will actually become more rewarding over time, not less. This is especially true of our love for God.

If you're consistent in spending time in God's presence, His character will infuse your whole life, and your capacity for love will increase. As you continue to pursue a relationship with Him, you'll find that your love for Him becomes more and more beautiful each day—because there's *always* one more thing to love about Him.

Lord, the more I get to know You, the more I love You. Amen.

Love That's Perfect

He is the Rock; his deeds are perfect. . . . He is a faithful God who does no wrong.

"Learn to relate to others through My Love rather than yours." Think about these words from *Jesus Calling*, by Sarah Young, in connection with the people in your life who are challenging to love.[3] We all know a few folks who are quick to push our buttons. Maybe they're especially high-maintenance, overbearing, or mean-spirited. Even those who are easiest to love have their moments!

Jesus' love can handle those people and those moments. When we feel too damaged to love someone in a healthy way, His love is perfect. When we're too exhausted to properly love someone with extreme needs, His love is tireless. When we feel too insecure to extend love for fear of getting hurt, His love is fearless.

When the act of loving feels difficult, it's okay to throw up your hands and say, "Lord, I can't do it. Help me relate to this person through Your love rather than my own." He'll be sure to answer . . . in love.

Lord, I'm so grateful that Your love is perfect, and that You're willing to love others through me. Please help me to love others through You. Amen.

Freedom

Listen, there's nothing wrong with zeal when you're zealous for God's good purpose.

Galatians 4:18 THE VOICE

Them: Where are you going?
You: Bible study.
Them: When are you going to get past this religious
phase?

Do you wish you could let hurtful comments like that roll off your back? If so, aspire to love God more each day and to be free from the fear of man. As you grow in these two things, you'll one day realize you've given up caring about what people think of your devotion to God.

Your friends may not approve of your choice to follow Jesus, but the truth is you'll *never* make a better choice! Dive so deep into your relationship with Jesus that your love for Him can't be swayed by what people think. Respect your friends, but don't worry if they disapprove of your devotion to God. You're grounded in a truth they don't yet see. Love them—and maybe one day you'll lead them to the best choice they'll ever make.

Lord, may I love You so much that no one can offend me or cause me to second-guess my devotion to You. Amen.

Love Gives Correction

Better a patient person than a warrior, one with self-control than one who takes a city.

Proverbs 16:32

Jammy and her sister, Tonya, didn't often disagree, but one day they had a heated argument. After Tammy cooled down, she decided to call Tonya and apologize when she got a text from Tonya's best friend: *You're a shrew! I don't know how Tonya puts up with you!* Suddenly, the altercation had escalated.

Some friendships include an unspoken agreement that if one gets offended, the other must get just as offended—or more so. They feed off one another's anger, mistaking it for loyalty: *If you're mad, I'm even madder!* But standing by a friend doesn't mean you must always agree with him or her; it simply means uninterrupted love. If your friend is offended by someone, and you know she needs to forgive that person, you have a responsibility to talk her down. True friends aren't afraid to gently correct one another. It's what love does.

I want to be a true friend, Lord. Help me to call my friends to a higher, not a lower, place! Amen.

God Loves the Details

You have stolen my heart with one glance of your eyes, with one jewel of your necklace.

Song of Songs 4:9

Do you ever feel weak in the knees when your sweetheart does some little thing—something so trivial that no one else even notices? Maybe you fall in love with her all over again every time she does that cute little sneeze. Maybe you still get butterflies when he holds the door open for you. Often, it's the tiniest details that make our hearts swell. So have you ever considered that God is smitten with the details too?

God might love the way I teach Sunday school, but surely He doesn't notice the way I sneeze.

He probably appreciates the time I helped the neighbors move, but surely there's nothing exceptional about opening a door for my wife.

Think again. God loves us completely—*everything* about us. After all, He formed us to His own liking. He fashioned us from head to toe in a way that's pleasing to Him. Right down to the last detail.

Lord, help me to believe beyond a shadow of a doubt that You love me from head to toe . . . and that You notice all the details. Amen.

Jehovah-Jireh

My God will meet all your needs according to the riches of his glory in Christ Jesus.

Philippians 4:19

When a carpenter builds a cabinet, that cabinet belongs to him until he gives or sells it to someone else. Likewise, because God created everything, all of creation belongs to Him. *You* belong to Him. Your children belong first of all to Him. Even, God says in Psalm 50:10, "every animal of the forest is [his], and the cattle on a thousand hills." God's storehouse is immense!

In Philippians 4:19, we read that God will meet *all* of our needs. In Hebrew, He's called *Jehovah-jireh*, which means "the Lord our Provider." We can ask God for absolutely anything we need, because He's sure to have whatever we need in His storehouse. So why does God want us to ask for what we need? Because by asking, we show that we believe, trust, and love Him.

A good father provides for his family because he loves them. As the perfect Father, God enjoys providing for us—because He loves us!

Lord, You are my Jehovah-jireh. Every good thing in my life comes from You and Your love—thank You! Amen.

True Success

When all is said and done, here is the last word: worship in reverence
the one True God, and keep His commands, for this is what God
expects of every person.

Ecclesiastes 12:13 THE VOICE

Merriam-Webster defines the word *success* as "the attainment of wealth, favor, or eminence."⁴ Do you agree? What does success look like to you? Are you living in such a way that, at the end of your life, you'll be able to say, "I lived a successful life"?

If you've been a Christian for even a short time, you already know that the principles of God's kingdom often contradict those of the world. This isn't to say that there's anything inherently wrong with wealth, favor, or eminence. Some devoted Christians have enjoyed all three. But in God's kingdom, the most successful believers are often poor, persecuted, and unpopular. But what do they all have in common? They love God.

If you're troubled about whether or not you're living a successful life, try saying this aloud: "If I come to the end of my days and the only thing I was known for was loving God, then my life was a beautiful success."

Thank You, Lord, for Your definition of success—to follow Your
Son, Jesus, and to love You with all my heart. Amen.

Leading with Love

When [Jesus] was alone with his disciples, he explained everything to them.

Mark 4:34 NLT

Every Saturday for ten months, the soup kitchen team leader had spooned great heaps of meat and vegetables onto the plates of her beloved guests. She loved her assignment so much that she didn't even mind the huge sink full of dirty dishes. But now she had a decision to make: a new group of volunteers had signed up for the summer. They were eager to pitch in. Was she willing to give up "her" spot so a new volunteer could learn how to serve?

If you've ever been in a leadership position, you know that—if you truly love those you lead as Christ loved His own followers—leadership is sacrificial. One of the most difficult lessons to learn is how to step back and let others do the job you love to do so they, too, can grow. Love chooses others above familiarity, comfort, and position. It nurtures those who are learning and passes the baton to those who are ready.

Help me, Lord, to make sacrifices for the people I lead. Remind me to step back and give them new responsibilities when they're ready. Amen.

Love and Monogamy

You belong to God, my dear children.

1 John 4:4 NLT

God's design for marriage is monogamy. Anything less causes extreme pain, division, and usually divorce. Most people want complete loyalty from their spouse. They're not willing to share the one they love, and rightly so.

So why should God expect anything less in His relationship with you? Do you think He's selfish for not just wanting but *demanding* all of you—your whole life, your dreams, your children, your marriage, your finances, your career, your plans, your past, and your future?

Sometimes we begrudge God for wanting all of us because we forget that we already belong to Him. And we might feel uncomfortable with the idea that He has a right to every detail of our lives because there's no telling what He might do!

Have you surrendered every detail of who you are to God? If not, what parts of your life are you still trying to control? Let go. Surrender to His love, and be free.

Lord, You have every right to every part of me and my life. Help me surrender all to You. Amen.

Love Versus Fear

"Do not let your hearts be troubled."

John 14:1

What if Jesus really meant what He said in John 14:1? What if we were to read this verse as more of a command than as words of comfort? What if we did the same with all those "fear nots" that occur repeatedly in the Bible?

We tend to read verses like these as mollifications: "There, there now. It'll be okay." But what if the message behind them is more like, "Stop being troubled. Stop being fearful—*now*." Can you imagine the freedom we'd experience if we obeyed God's directive and absolutely refused to entertain worry or fear? His love is big enough to swallow up all fear in our lives. Do you believe it?

Missionary Hudson Taylor did. He said, "Let us give up our work, our plans, ourselves, our lives, our loved ones, our influence, our all, right into [God's] hand; and then, when we have given all over to Him, there will be nothing left for us to be troubled about."5

I'm tired of being troubled and afraid all the time, Lord. I'm ready to obey Your command to "fear not." Set me free! Amen.

The Joy of Dependence

"Fear not, for I am with you; be not dismayed, for I am your God. I will strengthen you, yes, I will help you, I will uphold you with My righteous right hand."

Isaiah 41:10 NKJV

Picture a first grader fleeing from the meanest kid in class. This bully outweighs every other first grader and can throw a devastating punch. Our victim runs for his life until, finally, he rounds a corner—and there stands his big brother—fifteen years old and built like a lumberjack. Little brother knows big brother will take it from here.

As the little brother in this scenario, we should be just as happy to let God take over our lives. To truly obey God's directive to "fear not," we must hand Him *everything* that worries us. Then we can confidently lean back into His love until fear becomes a thing of the past.

As you learn to surrender, you'll become increasingly confident in God's love and strength. This goes against the ways of the world, where everyone clamors for independence and control. But think of it: you'll never again have to face your bullies alone.

Thank You for Your patience with me, Lord, as I've tried to run my own life and fight my own battles. Teach me to be utterly dependent on You. Amen.

Go in Peace

Then Jesus said to her, "Your sins are forgiven. . . . Go in peace."
Luke 7:48, 50

Have you ever spent time with someone who apologizes too much? She apologizes for the most minor infractions and mournfully rehashes old mistakes. She's even sorry for imagined offenses! Sometimes you just want to tell her to stop apologizing: "Clearly, I've got a lot more grace for you than you think I do! Even when you goof, I would never condemn you the way you seem to expect me to."

Does Jesus ever want to say the same to us? Repentance is a beautiful and holy thing. It's also *effective*. In other words, when we've confessed and repented for a sin, it's a done deal. Rehashing old offenses is exhausting and unnecessary—and it shows how little we believe God's promises. When He tells us (as He did the woman of Luke 7), "You're forgiven," we have no right to then say, "No, I'm not." Instead, let's receive the love and forgiveness of God and joyfully move on.

Lord, I know there are certain past sins I've rehashed a hundred times. I want to truly receive Your love and forgiveness; help me let them go. Amen.

Think unto Others

"In everything, do to others what you would have them do to you."
Matthew 7:12

One rainy day, your colleague dares to wear a pair of bright-orange wellies to work, and you decide she looks ridiculous. But a week later you wear a floppy red hat because you're fashionable and forward-thinking.

As your brother describes his latest weightlifting accomplishment, you think, *He really needs to get over himself.* A few days later, you post a selfie on Facebook and comment, "New running PR this morning! Go me!"

We're so hard on others. We might think we're doing a pretty decent job of living according to the golden rule, but loving as Jesus loves means we also *think* about others what we'd have them think of us. Our thought lives are so powerful—and, for good or for ill, we tend to act out what we think. So the next time you entertain a critical thought about someone, trade it immediately for a loving, uplifting one.

Clean up my thought life, Lord. Help me to be so inclined to think well of others that it becomes second nature. Amen.

Love and Money

Each of you should give what you have decided in your heart to give, not reluctantly or under compulsion, for God loves a cheerful giver.

2 Corinthians 9:7

Uh-oh. Here comes the collection basket. What should I put in it? No one's looking. Maybe I can get by with five dollars . . . or just one . . .

Is this what you think when the collection basket comes your way? Do you give the least you can get by with—or give only because someone might be looking?

Today's verse tells us that we should give cheerfully—not out of feelings of compulsion, and not reluctantly, but what we truly believe the Lord wants us to give. Giving to church, a ministry, or the disadvantaged is not just a command from God; it's a privilege. Because of donations, a church or ministry is able to do God's work here on earth. By giving to the poor, we're helping them pay bills, get health care, or buy food. That, too, is doing God's work. Best of all, our giving shows that we do, indeed, love our neighbors.

Lord, make me a cheerful giver. Help me to put into action my love for those around me. Amen.

Meet My Dad

Praise Him who lives on Zion's holy hill. Tell the story of His great acts among the people!

Psalm 9:11 THE VOICE

As Don approached his son Daniel's school on Bring a Parent Day, Daniel grabbed his hand and nearly dragged him into the building, all the while practically yelling at his classmates, "This is my dad! Hey, c'mere. This is my dad!" Don hushed him, but only half-heartedly. After all, few things are as great as when your kid absolutely adores being your kid.

Christians should be tremendously proud of their heavenly Dad. We should relish the thought of telling someone else about Him, of introducing Him to our friends. Do you love being His kid? Who have you introduced to your Dad? Keep in mind that God longs to be unashamedly loved and praised and adored by you. Invite someone to meet your heavenly Father, so he or she can learn to love and adore Him too.

I'm so proud to be Your child, Lord. I love that You're my Father, and I commit to tell as many people about You as I can. Amen.

Beloved and Holy

To all . . . who are loved by God and called to be his holy people:
Grace and peace to you.

Romans 1:7

Often we equate the word *holy* with "excessively pious" or, even worse, "self-righteous." Its true meaning, however, is twofold.

First, it means "set apart; for sacred (versus everyday) use." This doesn't mean "fancy," as in your only-for-special-occasions china compared to your everyday dishes. Instead, the meaning is closer to "outstanding in quality or rarity," as in, "Anyone can jump on the gossip bandwagon, but it takes holiness to build someone up when everyone else is tearing him down."

Secondly, according to Merriam-Webster.com, *holy* means "devoted entirely to the deity or the work of the deity."[6] This doesn't require a halo, a harp, or eight daily hours of contemplative prayer. A person can be radically devoted to Jesus while also raising seven kids, backpacking through Europe, or riding a Harley. If you belong to Jesus, you've already been set apart as His beloved. There's nothing run-of-the-mill about you. You're earmarked for God's use, outstanding in quality, and extraordinary. You are holy.

Lord, thank You for setting me apart as Your own. Let my life be a reflection of the holiness You have given me. Amen.

Plant a Little Love

The good deeds of the blameless pave a peaceful, productive path.

Proverbs 11:5 THE VOICE

Did you know you can use one little African violet leaf to grow a whole new plant? Even an inexperienced gardener can do it. Just cut a single fresh, mature leaf from a healthy plant and place it in a pot of light, porous soil. After about twelve weeks, you'll see that one or more tiny plants have sprouted from the leaf. These plantlets can then be rooted separately to produce new violets.

Sometimes it's shocking how much life can come from something very small and seemingly inconsequential. Love works the same way, multiplying heartily, sometimes because of a single kind deed. A devoted leader and his wife were sent on a five-day vacation by their congregation after one congregant put twenty dollars in a kitty and invited others to join her. That blessing, which will be remembered for decades, happened because one person planted a small gift of love that multiplied.

What gift of love will you plant today?

How can I increase love in the lives of the people around me, Lord? Show me, and I'll obey. Amen.

Love and Discipline

Blessed is the one whom God corrects; so do not despise the discipline of the Almighty.

Job 5:17

Isn't it annoying when a child screams in a grocery store because she wants something, but Mom says no? If Mom gives in, the child quiets down—until she wants something else. This mother might think she's showing the child love by giving in, but the Bible says otherwise: "Those who spare the rod of discipline hate their children. Those who love their children care enough to discipline them" (Proverbs 13:24 NLT). When a parent ignores a misbehaving child, she's telling her, "You're not important enough for me to take the time and effort to discipline you."

God practices what He preaches. He disciplines us not because He's angry with us but because He loves us beyond our imagination. He knows that without discipline, we'll become spoiled, unruly, rebellious children. Loving parents not only want to bless their children, but they also want to be a blessing. And God is the perfect loving Parent.

Lord, help me to gracefully accept discipline in my own life. Amen.

The Only One You Can Change

Be patient with each other, making allowance for each other's faults because of your love.

Ephesians 4:2 NLT

Have you ever thrown up your hands and blurted out, "I give up! You'll never change!"

What if you're all too right? What if you'll never be able to change the person you'd most like to change? What if he never adjusts his point of view or behavior?

There comes a time when you must stop exhausting yourself with trying to change someone else's behavior. That's also the time to ask yourself what *you* can do and how *you* should change. The answer might be as simple as, *I can choose to be patient and kind anyway.* Or your answer might need to be more drastic: *I can distance myself when she becomes verbally or emotionally abusive.* This doesn't equal a lack of love; it's being realistic. After all, an adult has the right *not* to change. It's then up to you to decide what your loving response will be.

Lord, please show me if there's anyone I need to stop trying to change. Help me to release him or her and to focus on my own behavior instead. Amen.

Entering God's Rest

Jesus said, "Come to me, all of you who are weary and carry heavy burdens, and I will give you rest."

Matthew 11:28 NLT

nxiety. Weight gain. Insomnia. Heart disease. Depression. Headaches. Memory loss. According to the Mayo Clinic, stress can cause all these problems and more.[7] Even so, in our culture we're so accustomed to being under pressure that we almost feel guilty when we're *not* stressed out! During the past few decades, Americans have come to equate being "stressed-out" with "successful," as though scurrying around on fast-forward for fifteen hours straight means you've had a productive day.

Sadly, we've so completely bought into the lie that stress equals success that we can even feel proud of how stressed we are. We'll even seek it out if we suspect we're not busy enough. In the meantime, we've forgotten how to enter into God's rest. The Lord has a place of calm and peace for us. A place where we can finally stop, be still, and relax in the truth that His love is enough.

Are you stressed-out? Enter God's rest.

I'm tired of always being in a hurry, Lord. Your love is enough. I choose to step into Your rest. Amen.

Your Relationship with Stress

"Peace I leave with you; my peace I give you. I do not give to you as the world gives. Do not let your hearts be troubled and do not be afraid."

John 14:27

To truly enter into God's rest, you might need to take a look at your relationship with stress. If you're like most people, stress is an abstract concept that you plan to deal with some-day. But to tackle the problem of stress, you must be honest about what role it plays in your life. For example, some people would do almost anything to be rid of stress, but others are uncomfortable with the thought of slowing down.

If you're ready to be rid of stress, first see it for what it is—toxic to your physical, mental, and spiritual health. Then change your values: learn to appreciate serenity, health, and rest more than those things that cause stress.

Love yourself enough to take care of yourself. Break up with stress by focusing on your relationship with God. When your priorities line up with His, you'll find that His love is enough and His rest is priceless.

Lord, please help me to say goodbye to stress and adjust my values so they line up with Yours. Amen.

Love Through Mentoring

To Timothy my true son in the faith: Grace, mercy and peace from God the Father and Christ Jesus our Lord.

1 Timothy 1:2

Did you read Homer's *Odyssey* in high school or college? If so, you might remember that when Odysseus left to fight in the Trojan War, his servant Mentor cared for Odysseus's son, Telemachus, during the hero's absence. For ten years, Mentor loved the boy as his own and taught him the skills he would need as a man.

This story is where we get the modern-day term *mentor*. Today, spiritual mentors are hard to find. Part of that may be because we have some misconceptions about mentoring. For example, we assume that the mentor must be older, but that's not necessarily true. Mentoring simply means passing on what you know. A typical mentor might be motivated by any number of things, but a spiritual mentor is first and foremost motivated by love.

Just imagine what might happen if each member of the body of Christ imparted some skill, some area of knowledge, or a measure of wisdom to someone else!

Please give me the confidence to mentor someone who needs to learn from me, Lord. And please send a mentor into my life so that I may learn as well. Amen.

The Natural Mentor

Even when I am old . . . do not forsake me, my God, till I declare
your power to the next generation.

Psalm 71:18

S ome people are natural mentors. They just seem to adapt to the role rather quickly. These people are priceless to the family of God because they're motivated by love and willing to sacrifice their time for those who are still growing and learning. Often, they're the spiritual mothers and fathers of a local church.

Are you a natural mentor? Ask yourself:

- *Do people seem to gravitate toward me when they need sound advice?*
- *Do I find it rewarding, rather than threatening, to help others succeed?*
- *Do I have specific knowledge that I'm willing to pass on?*
- *Am I excited about my work or ministry, and do I long to share that excitement?*
- *Do I find that interacting with others, including those who are different from me, is energizing?*
- *Do I find it easy to love people?*

How did you do? Are you ready to take someone under your wing?

Lord, I want to "declare your power to the next generation." Remind
me to continually give away all You've given me. Amen.

The Gift of Patience

As God's chosen people, holy and dearly loved, clothe yourselves
with compassion, kindness, humility, gentleness and patience.

Colossians 3:12

To be a great mentor, we must have love. And 1 Corinthians 13:4 tells us that "love is patient." So a great mentor must then be both loving and patient. When sharing knowledge with others, we all need to humbly remember that, no matter how much we know now, we all started at zero.

Do you struggle with patience? When you've explained a concept repeatedly and your protégé still doesn't get it, do you want to pull your hair out? You can't assume that someone new to the faith, or new to the concept you're explaining, will be able to jump in and instantly be fully up to speed. For example, starting a conversation with church words such as *grace* and *sanctified* might intimidate someone who has had little or no exposure to Christianity.

Slow down, remind yourself that love is patient . . . and remember that someone once took the time to teach *you.*

Lord, thank You for the people who've taught me what I know. Help
me share what I have learned in a loving and patient way. Amen.

JULY

....

Who shall separate us from the love of Christ?
Shall trouble or hardship or persecution or
famine or nakedness or danger or sword?

Romans 8:35

Trust and Forgiveness

Trusting a fool to convey a message is like cutting off one's feet or drinking poison!

Proverbs 26:6 NLT

"Love all, trust a few, do wrong to none," wrote William Shakespeare in *All's Well That Ends Well*. Notice that he didn't recommend trusting "all." In fact, he recognized that perhaps only a few people within one's circle of friends and family should truly be trusted. But doesn't loving someone mean you trust that person unconditionally? Not necessarily.

Maybe you've been mistreated repeatedly by the same person, yet she continues to expect your unconditional trust. The implication is that you haven't really forgiven her if you refuse to open yourself up to abuse again. Yes, Jesus expects Christians to forgive "seventy-seven times" (Matthew 18:22), but forgiveness is *not* the same as trust. Sometimes, wisdom demands that we use great caution with a manipulative individual.

When we refuse to punish a person for hurting us . . . when we hold no offense against him . . . when we're able to pray for him without bitterness in our hearts . . . *that's* forgiveness.

Lord, help me to quickly forgive those who hurt me, and to know when to be cautious, when to be vulnerable, and when to trust. Amen.

Timing Is Everything

It is wonderful to say the right thing at the right time!

Proverbs 15:23 NLT

No matter how much you love someone, conflicts are going to happen once in a while. If you want to do what's best for your relationship, talking it out is a must when feelings get hurt. However, you must also take timing into consideration. Sometimes a difficult conversation needs to happen, but the timing is wrong—in which case you must be patient and wait until the time is right.

Before you tackle a difficult conversation, ask yourself:

- *Am I emotionally stable enough to talk things out without letting my feelings get in the way?*
- *Is the other person emotionally ready to listen and work toward a solution?*
- *Do we both have enough time to have the conversation without feeling rushed?*
- *Am I willing to work toward reconciliation versus simply proving I'm right?*

If you answered no to any of these points, you might need to wait a little while before having that crucial conversation.

Lord, sometimes I get in a hurry, which adds to a problem. Help me to know the best time to have difficult conversations with my loved ones. Amen.

Be the Head

The LORD will make you the head, not the tail. If you pay attention to the commands of the LORD your God . . . and carefully follow them, you will always be at the top, never at the bottom.

Deuteronomy 28:13

In the good old days, it was a long-standing joke that when two people were needed to be in a horse costume, no one wanted to be the tail end. There was, it was thought, something degrading about being that part of an animal's body. From vaudeville to television, jokes about being "the south end of a northbound horse" were sure to elicit hearty laughter.

Even centuries before vaudeville, at the time of the Hebrew nation's exodus from Egypt, being the "tail" was equated with being something less desirable. The author of the book of Deuteronomy, Moses, told the Hebrew people (and, consequently, Christians today) that if they would carefully follow and obey God's laws, they'd certainly be "the head, not the tail" or "at the top, never at the bottom." This doesn't mean that God would love them (or us) more, but that He'd bless them (and us) more. Head or tail? Top or bottom? Make your choice today.

Lord, please help me to study Your Word and obey Your commands faithfully. And please bless me, so that I will never be the "tail." Amen.

Pardoned

Blessed is the one whose transgressions are forgiven, whose sins are covered.

Psalm 32:1

In the United States, being convicted of a felony means more than jail time for a criminal; it also means that certain civil liberties, such as the right to vote and the right to bear arms, are taken away. But a presidential pardon will reinstate all those liberties as though the crime had never been committed. Through the years, no president exercised his right to pardon criminals more than Franklin D. Roosevelt—pardoning 2,819 criminals![1]

Imagine the relief a person would feel upon hearing that he or she is finally free. But Christians have it even better. Whereas criminals are pardoned from jail time, we're pardoned from eternal suffering. That's the power of God's love. He gave Jesus so that we'd not only be freed from punishment for our sins, but also given full rights as children of God. On this day, when we celebrate the freedom of our country, thank God for your eternal freedom by telling others how they can be pardoned too.

A million thank-Yous, Lord, for pardoning me from the penalty of sin. Amen.

Yes or No?

Seek the LORD while he may be found; call on him while he is near.

Isaiah 55:6

Like Franklin D. Roosevelt, Andrew Jackson exercised his right to pardon convicted criminals. One day, he tried to pardon a postal clerk named George Wilson. Along with an accomplice, Wilson had been sentenced to death for committing murder and robbery. When President Jackson granted him a pardon, Wilson's sentence was reduced from the death sentence to twenty years. However, for reasons unknown, Wilson refused the offer. The Supreme Court decided that a pardon wasn't a pardon unless it was accepted, so Wilson's punishment was carried out, and he was eventually hanged.[2]

As wonderful as God's offer to pardon us and set us free from sin and its consequences is, He doesn't force anyone to take Him up on that offer. The thought that anyone would turn down the love of God and the liberty He grants is unfathomable, yet it happens all the time.

How about you? God has offered to wipe your record clean. Don't say no!

I humbly accept Your pardon, Lord, and I thank You for Your love, correction, instruction, and Word. Amen.

Knowing Him

For now we see only a reflection as in a mirror; then we shall see face to face. Now I know in part; then I shall know fully, even as I am fully known.

1 Corinthians 13:12

Have you ever gone to a window and opened the blinds so you could see more of a beautiful sunset? When the blinds are partially closed, you can see only some of the beauty; but when the blinds are fully open, you can see it all. In a similar manner, God reveals Himself to us only a little at a time. Here on earth, we can see Him only through what He's created. And we can know Him, but only as "a reflection as in a mirror"— through His written Word, the Bible.

Throughout biblical times, God revealed Himself to His followers slowly, because He knew that to reveal Himself all at once, would be too overwhelming. In the Bible, we're even told that if we were to see God face-to-face, we would die (Exodus 33:20). So because God loves us so much, He opens the blinds a little at a time.

Father God, please reveal more of Yourself to me each day. Thank You for Your written Word and for Your beautiful creation. Amen.

Two Thieves

In him we have redemption through his blood, the forgiveness of sins, in accordance with the riches of God's grace.

Three men hung on their crosses, facing imminent death. One man, Jesus, was completely innocent; one, a thief, was guilty and unrepentant; and the third, also a thief, was guilty, but he was pondering his fate. The "bad" thief began mocking Jesus. The "good" thief, however, was appalled. He looked at Jesus and said, "Remember me when you come into your kingdom" (Luke 23:42), thereby proclaiming that he knew Jesus to be Lord. That was all it took. "Today," Jesus declared, "you will be with me in paradise" (v. 43).

If you've ever redeemed a coupon, you know that *redeem* means part of your purchase price has already been paid. But when Jesus redeems us, we are completely redeemed. He fully paid our way into heaven by dying in our stead. All we need to do is believe that He's our Lord, repent, and obey. Because of His great love, He's done all the rest!

Lord, I do believe You're my Savior and the Lord of my life. I repent of my sins. Thank You for fully redeeming me. Amen.

Grace for Strangers

Do not show partiality.

We tend to give our closest friends a great deal of grace. Even when we argue with them, we know we'll get over it in time to go to the playoffs together. Ask anyone if there's anything that drives them crazy about their best friend, and they're likely to recite at least a short list—yet they're committed and loyal.

Why, then, are we so short-tempered when it comes to strangers? Perhaps it's because we're not invested in their lives. We find it inordinately easy to pass judgment on those we *don't* know. But the Lord disagrees. Like it or not, He's just as invested in that annoying person you just insulted as He is in you! That's why He instructs us to love our neighbors—whether we know them personally or not. God knows the value of every single human life.

Lord, remind me that a person's value isn't contingent on how well I know him or her. Help me to see all people as priceless. Amen.

God and Science

Speak to the earth, and it will teach you, or let the fish in the sea inform you. Which of all these does not know that the hand of the LORD has done this?

Job 12:8–9

Imagine, if you can, how many teaspoons of water are in the Atlantic Ocean. Now take that number and multiply it by eight. *That's* how many atoms are in one single teaspoon of water! Speaking of numbers, there are more than two hundred billion galaxies in the known universe. And a neutron star is so dense that one teaspoonful would weigh six billion tons.

Some people are wary of science for fear that it dilutes the faith of those who study it—but truth be told, the world of science is filled with one miracle after another. God created everything, and His fingerprints are everywhere. The existence of a loving God should thunder in your heart the more you learn about the world you live in. It's almost unbelievable that any scientist could suggest that there is no God.

Science and religion don't contradict each other; they complement each other. The love and the reality of God are written in the stars.

Awesome and mighty God, Your fingerprints are everywhere. I'm amazed by all that You have created. Amen.

Our Grudgeless God

Yet the LORD longs to be gracious to you; therefore he will rise up to show you compassion.

Isaiah 30:18

We've all heard of the Hatfields and McCoys because they had one of the most long-lasting (and infamous) feuds in history. The ruckus involved two families, led by patriarchs William Hatfield and Randolph McCoy, who resided on the West Virginia/Kentucky state line. The feud seems to have involved many issues, among them a prized hog, but whatever the central reason, the result was a grudge that lasted for decades.

People hold grudges; God doesn't. We tend to drag things out and make our enemy pay for his wrongs against us again and again; God doesn't. When you know you've rebelled against Him, be quick to confess—and He will be quick to forgive. There's no need to keep apologizing, yet many of us imagine that God is holding a grudge, expecting just a bit more contrition. But God doesn't do that.

Dear Lord, thank You for Your forgiveness, which is full and complete. Help me to set aside forgiven sins and move forward from this moment on. Amen.

Emotional Departure

"Return to me, and I will return to you," says the LORD. . . . "But you ask, 'How can we return when we have never gone away?'"

Malachi 3:7 NLT

Have you ever had a conversation with someone who seemed a million miles away? When you asked, "Did you hear anything I just said?" he answered, "Yes! Absolutely!" But he might as well have been sitting on the other side of town. He was with you physically, but, mentally and emotionally, he'd exited the building.

In today's verse, God asked the Israelites, who'd been worshiping idols, to return to Him. They responded, "What? We're right here! We haven't gone anywhere!" But they couldn't fool God; their hearts were long gone. They'd tired of loving Him. We can do the same thing to a loved one. It's quite possible to mentally pack our bags and leave a parent, son, daughter, spouse, or friend without ever leaving his or her presence. But if we realize and then humbly acknowledge what's happening, we can restore the relationship.

Have you "packed your bags" and left someone who needs you? Make it right today.

Lord, if there's someone I've offended by ignoring him or her, help me to return to that person, be honest, and make things right. Amen.

God Loves Your Voice

My dove in the clefts of the rock . . . let me hear your voice; for your voice is sweet.

Song of Songs 2:14

Through His Word, the Lord says to us, "Let me hear your voice." But do you truly believe that He loves to hear you pray? That He's concerned with whatever topics you choose to talk to Him about? That He's never bored by a conversation with you? That He never gets distracted and never stops paying attention?

The truth is that your prayers are precious to God, even when they're as simple as a child's. In fact, we have every reason to believe that simple is preferable to eloquent and flowery. The power of prayer is in the One we petition, not the flashiness of our words. If eloquence mattered, then children would have no audience with God, and we know that's not the case!

God thinks "your voice is sweet." Make Him happy today by taking time to talk to Him. Express your love for God with your voice.

I love that You love my voice, Lord! I commit to taking time each day to talk to You about the details of my life. Amen.

Eye Contact

You are beautiful, my darling, beautiful beyond words. Your eyes are like doves.

Song of Solomon 4:1 NLT

A sure sign of intimacy is eye contact. Lovers stare into each other's eyes. A mother's heart bursts with love when her baby looks into her eyes. Conversely, when we feel uncomfortable with someone, we break eye contact. Shame, anger, and fear cause us to look away.

"The eyes are the window to the soul," it's been said. So if we want to go deeper with God, eye contact is necessary. But how can we make eye contact with a God we can't see? By being completely vulnerable with Him. By laying down all our defenses and being transparent regarding our feelings, hopes, sorrows, joys, and fears.

Spend a few minutes in worship. Ask God to open your eyes—and your heart—to Him. If you start to feel a little too vulnerable, resist the urge to back away. No one loves you as much as God does. You're safe with Him.

Lord, I want to be as close to You as I possibly can. Teach me how to look into Your eyes. Amen.

Our Words

The one . . . whose tongue utters no slander . . . and casts no slur on others. . . . will never be shaken.

Psalm 15:2–3, 5

In the delightful Disney movie *Bambi*, the baby rabbit, Thumper, blurted out something unkind to Bambi. His mother scolded him, saying, "What did your father tell you?" Thumper sheepishly replied, "If you can't say something nice, don't say nothing at all."

What Thumper said to Bambi might well have been truthful, but it was also hurtful. Although we're always to speak the truth, that doesn't mean we're to say something that can hurt another person. Sometimes, as Mother Rabbit told her little one, it's better to say nothing at all. David, the author of Psalm 15, plainly told us that we must be very careful with our words. If we truly love others, we'll guard our tongues against saying anything that will offend them or harm someone's reputation. "Just as you want others to do for you, do the same for them" (Luke 6:31 HCSB). That's love.

Father God, please help me to control my tongue and always guard what I say. Let none of my words be hurtful or unkind. Amen.

Puppy Love

May the Lord guide your hearts into God's pure love and keep you headed straight into the strong and sure grip of the Anointed One.

2 Thessalonians 3:5 THE VOICE

Certain dogs have absolutely no sense of boundaries. To them, there's no such thing as "your space" and "my space"; it's all "our space." If you let one of these critters sleep on your bed, she'll sprawl across your legs so you can't move. The moment you get up, she'll roll into your spot just to get closer to your scent. She greets you with a flying leap, sits in your lap (even at seventy-five pounds), and wags her tail even when you scold her. She's so convinced you adore her, she simply can't get enough of you.

Imagine God's delight if we were all more like these love-drunk canines—if our ultimate goal in life was to be in His company at all times. What if we were so confident of His love for us that we couldn't get enough of Him?

If you want to please the Lord, drop your boundaries and invite Him into your personal space.

I invite You, Lord, to invade my personal space. Step right over any boundaries I might have. I want my life to be "our space"! Amen.

Now These Three

And now these three remain: faith, hope and love. But the greatest of these is love.

1 Corinthians 13:13

Have you ever tried to choose a paint color by looking at swatches in a hardware store? All those different shades of colors is enough to make your eyes cross! But just three primary colors—red, blue, and yellow—in a million various combinations of varying proportions create all the rest on the planet.

The Bible talks about three different primary ingredients: faith, hope, and love. According to 1 Corinthians, these three "last forever" (NLT). They are the virtues that "must characterize our lives" (THE VOICE). Every good thing—that is, every good word, every action that brings life and light into the world, every pure thought you think—all these come from some combination of faith, hope, and love. Think about it: is there even one wholesome act, word, or thought in your life that doesn't arise from your love for God or another human being; your hope in one of God's many promises; or your faith in Him?

Lord, life has meaning and purpose because of faith, hope, and love. May these three things characterize every aspect of my life. Amen.

Unreciprocated Love

"I have been grieved by their adulterous hearts, which have turned away from me."

Ezekiel 6:9

A mother sacrifices her career to stay home with her daughter, who won't even return her calls now that she's grown.

A husband strives to be a good partner only to discover his wife has been unfaithful.

A woman spends her savings to finance a rehab program for her sister, who then disappears . . . again.

Each of these people must ask: *Does the fact that the person I've loved so well now refuses to love me well in return change the way I feel about myself?*

Often, we measure our self-worth according to whether or not the love we extend to others is reciprocated. But this *can't* be an accurate gauge, no matter how real it feels. After all, how have humans responded to God's love, which He extends through Jesus? Some have fallen madly in love with Him, but others have spurned Him.

Don't measure yourself by the love of others; measure yourself by the love of God.

Lord, I choose to forgive the person who came to mind when I read this devotion. Please heal my heart and remind me that You've been there too. Amen.

Love and Emotions

As she stood behind him at his feet weeping, she began to wet his feet with her tears. Then she wiped them with her hair, kissed them and poured perfume on them.

Luke 7:38

This verse describes a woman who was feeling some strong emotions. The Pharisee in whose house this took place was appalled by the whole scene, especially because he knew she was just a common sinner. But Jesus explained that her tears and kisses were the result of gratitude for having been extravagantly forgiven.

Do you sometimes experience strong emotions when you're in God's presence? If so, are you ever unnerved by those emotions? Don't be. The Bible cautions against being led around by our feelings, yet it never discourages emotions in and of themselves. God isn't afraid of, surprised by, or troubled by our emotions; after all, He created them! There's nothing wrong with worship that elicits tears of joy or even laughter.

Emotions can't create love, but love does create emotions. Don't be afraid of being emotional with God.

Lord, thank You for emotions like affection, delight, surprise, gratitude, compassion, hope, joy, and love. I'm so grateful I find all of those things in You. Amen.

Our Hero

His eyes are like blazing fire.

Everyone loves a movie with a happily-ever-after ending. One in which the dashing young man sweeps the beautiful girl into his arms just as the credits start to roll. The plot usually involves an evil rival who tries to lure the girl away, so we all cheer when the hero finally crushes the bad guy.

Jesus is our happily-ever-after Hero. He stepped out of heaven to rescue us from an evil enemy bent on destroying us. He gave up absolutely everything in exchange for His bride. He's gallant, fearless, and utterly faithful. The Bible even depicts Him as riding on a white horse: "I saw heaven standing open and there before me was a white horse, whose rider is called Faithful and True" (Revelation 19:11).

Rejoice! Jesus is your hero, His love is unshakable, and He's got a happily-forever-after ending planned for you.

Jesus, You truly sweep me off my feet! Help me to turn to You whenever I need a hero—and even when I don't. Amen.

The Lord Our Husband

"In that day," declares the LORD, "you will call me 'my husband.'"

Hosea 2:16

The apostle Paul. John the Baptist. Amy Carmichael. John Stott. Dietrich Bonhoeffer. Corrie ten Boom.

What do these spiritual giants have in common? They were unmarried.

Sadly, many people, even in the church, have bought into the idea that marriage is the be-all and end-all, and that singleness is somehow "less than." But this is ridiculous, especially considering that Jesus was also on that singles list!

The Lord invites us to know Him as "Husband." You might ask, "What about physical touch and audible conversation?" True—literal touch and audible conversation aren't possible in a romance with one's Creator, and it's natural to long for them. Still, God promises to fulfill everyone who pursues Him, married *or* single: "[God] will satisfy your needs in a sun-scorched land and will strengthen your frame. You will be like a well-watered garden, like a spring whose waters never fail" (Isaiah 58:11). There's no such thing as the solitary life when you walk with God.

I receive by faith, Lord, Your perfect love that always satisfies. With You, I know I am never alone. Amen.

Perfect Union

Make this your one purpose: to revere Him and serve Him faithfully with complete devotion because He has done great things for you.

1 Samuel 12:24 THE VOICE

Marriage is always a work in progress. Every marriage is flawed because every person in a marriage is flawed. Even the kindest, most noble spouse is weak and broken. And though no marriage is perfect, that relationship does point us to the perfect union between Jesus and His bride.

God's love for us is all-consuming and flawless. And He invites us into a deep, personal relationship that is the shining example for all our other relationships—even marriage. It is selfless, giving, and forgiving. And so should we be in all our relationships—whether it's with our spouse, a friend, a family member, a coworker, or our neighbor across the street.

Whether you're married or single, "make this your one purpose: to revere [God] and serve Him faithfully with complete devotion because He has done great things for you."

My heart always longs to know You better, Jesus. I accept the absolutely perfect love You offer me and will try to imitate it with the people in my life. Amen.

Stormy Weather

Neither height nor depth, nor anything else in all creation, will be able to separate us from the love of God that is in Christ Jesus our Lord.

Romans 8:39

Hurricanes, tornados, volcanoes, tsunamis, earthquakes . . . sometimes the natural storms of life seem to say that the Lord is upset with us. But Romans tells us clearly that nothing "in all creation" can separate us from God's bottomless love. There are times when these storms hit us personally—the roof is torn off the house, the basement floods, the beautiful spruce in the backyard is flattened—and it might be difficult to believe God still loves us. But consider this: would Jesus have died for your sins if He didn't love you with an extravagant, personal love?

Sometimes God tests us and builds our character through personal storms, but often they're just the result of a sin-filled world. When God banished Adam and Eve from Eden, He warned them that life in this world would be difficult. But He also promises us that life in the next world will be glorious for His children.

Thank You, Lord, for loving me so much that nothing in all creation can separate me from Your love. Amen.

I Love You This Much

The celestial realms announce God's glory; the skies testify of His hands' great work.

Psalm 19:1 THE VOICE

Most of us would be quick to acknowledge that all of creation "speaks" of God—that it announces His majesty and splendor. But how many of us realize that creation also declares His love for us? Because we're mere humans, we couldn't handle God revealing His love for us in all its divine fullness, so He speaks to us through His creation.

If you've ever stepped outside your door on a brilliant, seventy-degree day after a week of cold rain and thought you were going to explode with joy—or if you've ever choked back tears at the sight of a canyon, a field, a forest, or a waterfall—those were God's ways of telling you how much He loves you. Just imagine someone stretching his arms out and shouting, "I love you *this* much!" That's what God does with each sunrise, each sunset that stretches across a never-ending sky. What will you say to Him in reply?

I see the works of Your hand, and I hear You, Lord. You're telling me how much You love me, and my heart is about to burst in reply. Amen.

I Love You Too

You should love Him, your True God, with all your heart and soul,
with every ounce of your strength.

Deuteronomy 6:5 THE VOICE

Just as God expresses the extent of His love for us through the wonders of His creation, we can express our love for Him through a selfless and servant-minded life.

I love you, God says, as He splashes the night sky with a million stars.

I love you too, we say, as we forfeit an evening of relaxation to cook supper for a sick mother-in-law.

I love you, God says, as He sends a raincloud to cool a stifling August afternoon.

I love you too, we say, as we forgive our teenager for words spoken in haste.

I love you, God says, as He scatters a thousand wildflowers across an open field.

I love you too, we say, as we refuse to fret and worry over a company lay-off.

Family life, marriage, work, friendships, seasons of joy, seasons of suffering—they all offer daily opportunities to follow, to obey, to say . . . "I love You, God."

Through every detail of my daily life, I want to say that I love You,
too, Lord! Amen.

Concrete or Conceptual?

. . . to take a fresh breath and to let God renew your attitude and spirit.

Ephesians 4:23 THE VOICE

Some people tend to think in concrete ways. They like facts, figures, specifics. They're not into fluff and instead talk in terms of calculations, parameters, and practical details.

Others are more conceptual, relying on intuition and imagination. They're creative and prone to gut feelings; they like the big picture, metaphors, and language that's descriptive and emotional.

A concrete thinker will buy you running shoes for your birthday, while the conceptual thinker will rent *Chariots of Fire* and feed you chocolate cake. A concrete thinker will pick up everything on your shopping list, but spend an extra twenty minutes finding the best prices; a conceptual thinker will forget there *is* a list, but grab a bouquet of flowers at the checkout.

Most people prefer to be loved in a way that's closer to their own style, but neither way is wrong or less loving. Learn to appreciate the gift of love—whichever way it's shown.

Thank You, Lord, for giving me the capacity for concrete and conceptual thought. Help me to find a balance between the two. Amen.

Planters and Waterers

So neither the one who plants nor the one who waters is anything,
but only God, who makes things grow.

1 Corinthians 3:7

One of the surest ways to break the bonds of love between members of a church—or even the body of Christ as a whole—is to compare gifts and callings. The moment we start doing that is the moment we begin to see one another as competitors.

In today's verse, Paul explained that no one has anything to brag about except God. Without Him, none of us would be able to take a single breath, let alone use our gifts.

If we were to join forces and plant a community garden, would we argue that the guy who planted the zucchini seeds was more important than the woman in charge of the garden hose? Of course not. If you're a planter, don't despise the waterer. If you pull weeds, you don't compete with the one who spreads the fertilizer. We're in this together . . . all together in the love of God.

Lord, bless the planters and the waterers of Your kingdom. Help me
to love my task and do it well, whatever it may be. Amen.

The Facets of God

"Be holy, because I am holy."

The most popular cut of diamond by far is the Round Brilliant Cut, with 58 facets. But there's also a diamond with 144 facets! Imagine turning it in the light to see its many brilliant surfaces, each one more beautiful than the last. Sometimes we refer to God's countless characteristics as *facets*. But is there a facet of God you don't like as much as the others, or that makes you uncomfortable?

We can't even begin to know God or see Him correctly if we focus on just one or two of His qualities. God is love; He's compassion and faithfulness and grace. But He's also justice, judgment, holiness, and purity. Often we squirm at the mention of these latter traits because they tend to highlight our own sin and frailty.

When it comes to that divine trait you're not so comfortable with, do your best to learn more about it. God is perfect, and every facet of Him deserves your love!

Lord, I don't want to cherry-pick the parts of You that I think I need. Show me more of who You are today. Amen.

Opposites or Not?

There is no fear in love. But perfect love drives out fear, because fear has to do with punishment.

1 John 4:18

Straight and *crooked*; *up* and *down*; *dusk* and *dawn*; *late* and *early*; *weak* and *strong*; *neat* and *messy*. These are all opposites. To most people, *love* and *wrath* seem like opposites, too—but the two are very connected.

Wrath is one of those facets of God we don't like to think about. But that's because we tend to think of wrath in human terms: imperfect, raging, and sometimes misdirected.

Do you believe that God is love, as He says He is? If so, then even if you can't understand the concept of wrath, you *can* trust that, since God is perfect love, even His wrath is a product of love. And here's the bottom line for anyone who belongs to Jesus: "Perfect love drives out fear"—even the fear of wrath. Why? Because Jesus took our punishment, making a way for us to escape God's wrath. We are free!

I'm amazed, Lord, at how Your love prevails over everything, even my sin. Thank You for sending Jesus so that I don't need to fear a thing. Amen.

Love and Stuff

"When he found a pearl more beautiful and valuable than any jewel he had ever seen, the jeweler sold all he had and bought that pearl."

Matthew 13:46 THE VOICE

We read the story of the pearl of great price metaphorically, but what if its lesson (that gaining God's kingdom is worth forfeiting everything else) were more literal for some people than for others? We're quick to agree that God appoints certain people to be wealthy so they can finance the kingdom, but doesn't it also stand to reason that some are called to simplicity and minimalism?

How much do you love your stuff? A person can be very possessive of what she owns—even if it doesn't amount to much. On the other hand, the more you own, the more you have to lose if Jesus should ask you to downsize and follow Him. Thus, one of the loveliest things about refusing to accumulate stuff is that you'll have less to give up if He calls you to a more sacrificial life.

Is it time for you to simplify so you can focus on the pearl of Christ?

Would You like me to simplify, Lord? Would I be better able to love and serve You if I had less stuff? Help me to follow Your leading. Amen.

More Than You Can Give

[God] is not served by human hands, as if he needed anything.
Rather, he himself gives everyone life and breath and everything else.

Acts 17:25

Remember when you were a child and your parents ran out of ideas about how to entertain you on those long summer days? If you were lucky, your family owned one of those inexpensive kiddie pools and a couple of sieves or colanders. You'd spend hours filling them with water and then watching it slip through the holes, creating tiny rain showers.

Some people are like sieves. You try and try to love them well, but you just can't seem to give them what they need. (It's probably more accurate to say that they need more than you—or anyone else—can give.) Sometimes such a person can drain you. You might feel as if they're smothering you or even obsessing about you.

Don't feel guilty about putting a little distance between yourself and an inordinately needy person. God will use the opportunity to show that person that only He can meet his or her every need.

Lord, please show me if I've been trying to fulfill a role in someone else's life that only You can fill. Amen.

Breathtaking

After this I looked, and there before me was a door standing open in heaven.

Revelation 4:1

Have you ever taken a photo of something breathtaking only to be disappointed with it later? Maybe you stood at the foot of Mount Rainier, or gazed at the Chicago skyline late at night, and the sight overwhelmed you almost to the point of tears—but the photo just didn't capture what you saw. All you could say is, "It was so much more beautiful than this. I guess you had to be there."

We know heaven will be good because God has told us certain things about it, but the real thing will take our breath away. We might dare to dream big, and yet we still cannot fathom what God has prepared for us because of His unspeakable love. He's created a heaven for His beloved children, and it's far more than we could ever dream. But one day, we'll finally be there—and it'll be so much more than we ever imagined.

As the song says, Lord, I can only imagine what heaven will be like. Thank You for preparing a place for me! Amen.

AUGUST

....

Jonathan had David reaffirm his oath out of love
for him, because he loved him as he loved himself.

1 Samuel 20:17

Mosaic

*For we are God's masterpiece. He has created us anew in Christ
Jesus, so we can do the good things he planned for us long ago.*

Ephesians 2:10 NLT

For almost thirty years, Raymond Isidore, a middle-age lab-
orer living in Chartres, France, covered his home (including
garden, furniture, and floors) with broken ceramic tile and
crockery. The result is a breathtaking mosaic visited by thirty
thousand tourists every year. If you were to look at any single
piece of tile, it would seem to you a worthless fragment, something
to be tossed in the garbage can. But stand back at a distance, and
you'd see a stunning still life, landscape, portrait, or geometric
design.[1]

Each stone in a mosaic is like a piece of your life. This task,
that friendship, this career, that sorrow—they are all working together even though you can't see the pattern yet. Every
moment counts, no matter how mundane or grand. And what
molds all those fragments together? The love of God. It gives
purpose and brings harmony to all the little pieces of life . . . to
create a masterpiece.

*I trust that You have all the pieces of my life in Your hand, Lord.
Thank You for Your love that makes it all fit together. Amen.*

Cheerful Generosity

You will be enriched in every way for all generosity, which produces thanksgiving to God.

2 Corinthians 9:11 HCSB

The smiling mother gave her small son two pennies to put into the church collection basket as it came by. The boy clutched one penny in each hand. When the basket had passed, the boy shouted out, "Ha-ha! I kept one!" and triumphantly showed everyone his hoarded penny.

An oft-repeated expression heard today is "You can't out-give God." Although this isn't a precise quote from the Bible, it's certainly true and has been proven again and again. No one is as generous as the Lord. However, knowing that He rewards our generosity shouldn't be our motive for faithful giving. Instead, we should be deeply grateful when we have the means to be generous. Note in the verse above that "generosity . . . produces thanksgiving to God." If you love God, love your church, and love the people whom your money will serve, you'll give—cheerfully, willingly, and thankfully.

Lord, teach me to give not just because I feel I have to, but because I want to and to be thankful that I can. Amen.

Living at Peace

If it is possible, as far as it depends on you, live at peace with everyone.

Have you heard the story of the little boy who was relegated to the time-out chair for five minutes for being too rowdy? As he grudgingly climbed into his seat, he said, "I might be sitting down on the outside, but I'm still standing up on the inside!"

At first glance, Romans 12:18 might seem to be telling us to avoid conflict, try not to fight with others, do our best to resolve arguments, and so on. And these are certainly good things to do. But what if this verse isn't just about fighting, but about keeping peace *internally*? We can look peaceful and foster peace among others on the outside, while resentfully standing up on the inside—stewing while pasting a smile on our face. Living at peace requires that we genuinely let offenses go so that our smiles are real, and the love we feel for others is deep in our hearts.

I acknowledge that sometimes I paste on a smile while I'm still angry. Help me to be quick to "sit down on the inside." Amen.

Invisible Illness

Brothers and sisters, pray for us.

1 Thessalonians 5:25

Fibromyalgia. PTSD. Chronic exhaustion. Thyroid disease. These are all invisible illnesses. When we see a cast on a leg, a scar after a surgery, or a wound from an injury, we easily relate—and we're quicker to empathize and understand the sufferer's limitations. But those who deal with invisible illnesses don't necessarily look sick and, thus, might not receive the compassion they need.

In the same way, someone who has lacked genuine love in his or her life (perhaps through abuse or neglect) will often suffer from deep inner wounds no one else can see. Friends and family might bear the brunt of the sufferer's anger or depression while being clueless as to what's really going on. If you've had to exercise unending patience lately with a friend, family member, or coworker, remember that he just might be reacting to a chronic lack of love. A little loving compassion might go a long way.

Help me to be quick to feel compassion and empathy for those whose scars I can't see, Lord. Amen.

Loving the Trailblazer

Acknowledge those who work hard among you, who care for you in the Lord. . . . Hold them in the highest regard in love because of their work.

1 Thessalonians 5:12–13

No doubt you've heard of Magellan, Marco Polo, and Edmund Hillary, but what do you know about the people who loved and supported them? If you said, "Nothing," you're in good company. These men and others like them have changed the world, achieving what seemed impossible, while those who supported, prayed for, and loved them remain anonymous.

Is there a trailblazer in your life? Does your best friend lead a Christian nonprofit? Does your son or daughter take part in foreign missions? Maybe you feel as though life is passing you by while your loved one's is meaningful and energizing. But have you considered that your greatest ministry might be to love and support that person?

Some are called to be trailblazers, and others are called to care for the trailblazers. Without your loving sacrifices, your world-changer might not be able to fulfill his or her mission. What a noble calling!

Thank You, Lord, for the privilege of loving _____ so he or she can, in turn, love and serve many others. Amen.

Blow the Roof Off

All glory to God, who is able . . . to accomplish infinitely more than we might ask or think.

Ephesians 3:20 NLT

We've all heard the saying, "When God shuts a door, He opens a window." But might this be selling God short? Think about it: a window is smaller than a door, so the implication is that God will bring something in your life to an end only to give you a *lesser* blessing. But because God loves to take His children to new heights and give them greater and greater blessings, He'll often bring something to an end so He can offer you something *better*—perhaps far beyond what you even imagined.

God won't *always* trade something good for something astounding, but dare to believe that sometimes He will! He'll close a door, but instead of opening a window, He'll blow the roof off, leaving you standing there, looking straight up at a clear, endless sky. He'll open up blessings so big and wide you'll hardly be able to catch your breath. Will you dare to believe it?

I choose to believe that You're about to blow the roof off in an area of my life where You recently closed a door. Thank You, Lord! Amen.

Stability

Be on your guard; stand firm in the faith; be courageous; be strong.
1 Corinthians 16:13

If you've ever watched a high-rise go up, you've probably seen construction workers set rebar (short for *reinforcing bar*) into the structure's foundation. Rebar is made of steel and helps carry the load of the building and cut down on cracking in the concrete. It's the stuff that holds a foundation together and brings stability.

The church today needs some "spiritual rebar." Sadly, stability is a rare thing these days. There's so much change and compromise happening all around that even Christian leaders are vacillating in their principles. If you're a leader, never forget that your crew—whether a congregation of hundreds or a family of four—needs you to love them enough to stand fast for what the Bible says. The double-minded leader inadvertently keeps his charges off balance. So don't be swayed. Put your confidence in the love of God, hold fast to *His* principles, and lead with boldness.

Lord, I've taken hold of truth, and I won't let go no matter what.
Help me to lead well and with stability. Amen.

One by One

You who seek God, let your hearts revive.

Psalm 69:32 ESV

f you grew up in church, you're probably familiar with the word *revival*. To many people, revival means renting a large tent and gathering as many people as possible for several days of meetings with a special speaker. It's always good to see many people come to the faith at once, but is this the only way revival can take place?

Imagine what would happen if thousands of residents of the same town were personally revived in their hearts by the love of God. What if each one experienced the spark of a renewed love for God, His people, and His purposes? Have you ever been to a concert where everyone turned his or her phone light on? The whole place glowed with light, didn't it? In reality, each light was rather small, but together, the effect was amazing. So it is with single hearts that have been revived: together, they can change a whole city, or even a nation.

Please bring revival to my town, Lord, and let it start with my own heart. Amen.

Life from Death

"I am the resurrection and the life. The one who believes in me will live, even though they die."

John 11:25

Before March 1980, driving drunk had little to no legal consequences. All that changed when Candy Lightner's daughter was killed by a repeat offender. In the aftermath of that tragedy, Lightner founded MADD, Mothers Against Drunk Driving. This action had a ripple effect, and countless lives have been spared because of Lightner's efforts.[2]

Many times, death brings life. We shy away from talk of death, yet that's what redemption is all about: Jesus died so we can live eternally. We, in turn, die to ourselves so we can know the love of Christ and then offer it to others. It might seem unfair or even cruel that the best sort of life is available only through death, but it's actually love—the love of Christ—that makes it possible. One day everything will make sense, and death will be a thing of the past.

I can hardly wait, Lord, until death has no power over anyone. Until then, teach me to die to myself so I can truly live. Amen.

Listen Up

My child, listen to what I say, and treasure my commands.

Dad: Mom and I have a meeting tonight, and we need you to watch your brother, okay?

Daughter: Hmm . . . how about if I do the laundry instead?

Dad: We could definitely use help with that, but tonight we'd like you to babysit.

Daughter: I think I'll mow the yard.

Dad: Wonderful—but tonight you'll watch your brother, right?

Daughter: Umm . . .

This sounds ridiculous, but isn't it much like the conversations we sometimes have with God when it comes to subjects that make us uncomfortable? Maybe He's asking you to stay pure before marriage, but you're offering other works as compensation while hoping He doesn't notice you're inching closer and closer to sin.

Loving God means obeying Him (John 14:15). Has the Lord been trying to talk to you about a certain issue? Have you been offering to do everything *except* that one thing He's asking of you? Stop changing the subject. Listen to God.

Lord, I confess that I've been ignoring You on the issue of _____.
I do love You; please help me to obey. Amen.

Learn from the Father

Don't let anyone look down on you because you are young, but set an example for the believers in speech, in conduct, in love, in faith and in purity.

1 Timothy 4:12

In January 2012, Laura Dekker became the youngest person to sail around the world solo—at the age of sixteen. She was just fourteen when she began her voyage. Naturally, people were shocked that her parents would allow her to do such a thing. But right or wrong, she succeeded because, thanks to her father, she had countless hours of experience under her belt before she set sail. In fact, Laura was born on a boat. As a child, she was coached by her father, who gave her plenty of free rein to learn sailing firsthand.[3]

If you're a young Christian, don't let anyone imply that you can't live a victorious Christian life. Stay close to the Father. Learn from Him. You might be far more equipped to live a spiritually successful, holy life than some people who've sat in a pew for decades. Love the journey, and love and respect your Captain. He'll keep you on course.

Thank You, Lord, for being willing to use people of every age to accomplish Your purposes on earth. I am eager to see how You will use me. Amen.

Our Loving Gardener

The LORD will surely comfort Zion . . . he will make her deserts like Eden, her wastelands like the garden of the LORD. Joy and gladness will be found in her.

Isaiah 51:3

They say that gardening is both the oldest profession and hobby, and the book of Genesis agrees. In chapter 2, we read that "the LORD God took the man [Adam] and put him in the Garden of Eden to work it and take care of it" (v. 15). Imagine what a delightful job that must have been in the days before root rot, drought, and weeds!

Our God is the best gardener of all, however. He described Himself as not just having a garden (see today's verse) but as tending it as the ultimate Gardener. When His church and His people are dry and thirsty, He brings life: "*Like a devoted gardener*, I will pour *sweet* water on parched land, streams on hard-packed ground; I will pour My spirit on your children and grandchildren—and let My blessing flow to your descendants" (Isaiah 44:3 THE VOICE). When you feel lifeless, ask the Lord to refresh you with joy and gladness.

I am thirsty for You, Lord. Break up my fallow ground and saturate me with Your loving presence. Amen.

Let Go

Those who cling to worthless idols turn away from God's love for them.
Jonah 2:8

Have you ever been around a toddler when it's time for her to trade in her old, ratty, smelly, stained blankie for a new one? Everyone knows its time, but Baby Girl has her own ideas. The moment Mama tries to snag the vile thing, the toddler shrieks like a spider monkey. It's hers, and she's not letting go without a fight.

Sometimes we're the same way about a favorite dysfunction. Whether fear, greed, cattiness, or jealousy, it's damaging our relationships and sowing discord instead of love. But it's familiar, like a longtime (albeit toxic) friend—or a tattered security blanket—so we clutch it to our chest.

We have to get past the mind-set that we have a right to our dysfunctions. We have no more right to them than we do to any other sin. Do you want healthy, loving relationships more than you want to hold on to your issues? Release them and grab grace instead.

Help me, Lord, to completely release into Your hands the issues and hang-ups that stand between me and loving relationships—right here and now. Amen.

What's at Stake?

Keep yourselves in God's love as you wait for the mercy of our Lord Jesus Christ to bring you to eternal life.

Jude v. 21

Two friends swore off processed sugar on the same day—but for different reasons. Both were determined to succeed, but four weeks later Friend 1 was eating Pop-Tarts and chocolate milk for breakfast again, while Friend 2 had learned to enjoy rolled oats and almonds. When asked about the difference in their results, Friend 1 said, "I got bored with it." Friend 2 explained, "I'm hypoglycemic, so my health was at stake. I couldn't afford to cheat."

Same initial zeal, but totally different results. We see this with Christianity too. If someone comes to Jesus simply because it seems like a good idea at the time, she'll likely abandon her faith when the going gets tough or boredom sets in, no matter how much zeal she had in the beginning. But the person who realizes what's really at stake will "stick."

So, what *is* at stake? Everything! Not only eternal life, but *this* life lived with God—or without Him.

Lord, even when I don't feel very zealous, I refuse to live a single day without Your love. Amen.

Upside Down

"Just as you sent me into the world, I am sending them into the world."

John 17:18 NLT

Jesus: Go into all the world and preach the gospel to all creation [Mark 16:15].

Peter (to John): Did you hear that? Go into "all the world"? Preach to "all creation"?

John: Has He forgotten there are not many of us?

Okay, so this scene is speculative. But do you ever feel as if the Lord is being unreasonable in what He expects of you or your spiritual family? Maybe He's forgotten that your church's finances only stretch so far. Or that your circle is passionate for Jesus but too small to change a whole city.

What *you* are forgetting is that a few people who love God fervently are far more effective than five thousand who are lukewarm. In Acts 17, a small group of disciples was accused of having "turned the world upside down" (Acts 17:6 HCSB). Do you believe you and your circle, no matter how small, can turn your world upside down? With God, you can!

May my little group be obedient to Your call, Lord! Help us change our world in Jesus' name. Amen.

Pain and Passion

He consoles us as we endure the pain and hardship of life so that we may draw from His comfort and share it with others in their own struggles.

2 Corinthians 1:4 THE VOICE

Many people would agree that bats are frightening and ugly. But what's even worse than a bat? Bat guano. Nevertheless, bat guano is in high demand, especially by organic farmers. Collecting the stuff is backbreaking work (and distasteful!), but in some regions, it's crucial to agriculture. When used as fertilizer, guano produces vegetables that are bursting with nutrients—overflowing with life itself, you might say.

It's astounding that something so offensive can yield something so valuable. Pain can be like that too. Physical pain, sorrow, grief—the things we avoid at all costs—often result in a deeper love, even passion, for God. Yes, pain is ugly, detestable, fearful. Yet many Christians will testify that it brought them closer to God's heart. You don't have to understand how it all works; just find comfort in knowing that, if you continue to trust God, the pain you feel *will* be transformed into contentment, wisdom, even joy.

I trust You, Lord, that the pain I experience will lead me to an even deeper love for You and others. Amen.

A Little Help from Your Friends

If one of them falls, the other can help him up.

Ecclesiastes 4:10 THE VOICE

Imagine you and a loved one are walking across a construction site. He steps a little too close to a deep pit and falls in. He's hurt and bleeding but still mobile. Thankfully, you spot a rope ladder and toss it down. "Climb up!" you shout. But he answers, "No, I don't want to bother you. I'll figure this out myself. Go on without me."

Are you like that person? Do you refuse to allow anyone to help you during a crisis? If so, know this: you can bless the ones you love by letting them love you back! Let them lend a hand. If you isolate yourself when you're in pain, this not only prolongs your suffering, but it also hurts the people who love you. Don't let the enemy tell you that you mustn't let anyone find out you're not perfect. They already know you're not! When they offer help, be humble enough to accept it.

Lord, thank You for the people in my life who love me. Give me a nudge when I'm stubborn, and remind me to accept help. Amen.

What You Were Made For

Those who worship Him will possess everything important in life.

Psalm 34:9 THE VOICE

What if you were making dinner with a friend, and he or she was trying to open a can with a toaster or peel a potato with a spoon? You'd say, "What are you doing? That's not what that's made for!"

Certain things are created for certain purposes. Rabbits don't try to fly, and eagles don't try to hop around on the ground, because that would be silly and ineffective. As people, we were made to worship our Creator. Making anything else the focus of our lives is silly and ineffective too. If we don't regularly engage in worship, we ache for it (whether or not we realize that's what we're longing for). In our frustration, we might act out in ways that leave us feeling empty. But when we step into God's presence, it resets us and realigns us with His love.

Have you been out of sorts? Draw closer to God through worship—it's what you were made for.

I'm Your creation, Lord, and You're my Creator. I was made for You alone. Amen.

Float

Then the angel showed me the river of the water of life, as clear as crystal, flowing from the throne of God and of the Lamb.

Have you ever jumped into an inner tube and floated down a river on a summer day? When an object—like an inner tube—is placed in water, it displaces the water around it. Meanwhile, the water pushes upward (upthrust). If the upthrust is more than the weight of an object, the object floats. Since the weight of an inflated inner tube is far less than the upthrust of the water, you can float all day with virtually no effort.

God is like a river. He has the power to take us where we need to be *if* we let Him. His "river of the water of life" flows continually; we just need to get into the flow. This doesn't mean the God-life is effortless or problem-free; rather, the power of God—the upthrust—is strong enough to keep us from ever sinking. Trust Him, relax into His love for you, and . . . float.

Lord, I'm tired of striving. Teach me to relax and just float in the river of Your love. Amen.

Under Jesus' Wings

*"Jerusalem, Jerusalem . . . how often I have longed to gather your
children together, as a hen gathers her chicks under her wings."*

Matthew 23:37

People who raise chickens know that a mother hen won't run
around collecting her babies; instead, she'll squat down
and spread her wings, and a cluster of baby chicks will come
running, chirping and cheeping, to snuggle under her wings,
which she then wraps protectively around them. *How lovely!* you
might think. *They must feel so safe and secure, so loved.*

In today's verse, Jesus was lamenting the fact that though
He'd offered His loving care and protection, the people had
turned their backs on Him. Thankfully, Jesus never stops offering. Even today, He does what He did then: spreads His wings
and waits for His flock to take refuge in Him. But just as the
people did so long ago, far too many of us still turn away, pre-
ferring to explore the world's temptations.

Have you accepted the Lord's offer of love and shelter?
There's no place as safe and secure as under His wings.

*Dear God, thank You for Your loving offer to shelter me in Your tender
embrace, and to guide and protect me all the way to heaven. Amen.*

Above the Smog

He raised Christ from the dead and seated him at his right hand in the heavenly realms.

Ephesians 1:20

Air pollution: it's smelly, unhealthy, and ugly. Sometimes called smog (a word created in the 1950s in London by blending *smoke* and *fog*, both of which had settled over the city at the time), it can even be lethal.[4]

Do you ever feel as if you're surrounded by your own, personal cloud of smog? Does your smog look a whole lot like depression, stress, loneliness, or boredom? The love of God will lift you out of your polluted atmosphere. Today's verse tells us that Jesus lives in a pure, heavenly place, and Ephesians 2:6 tells us that our spirit is already there with Him: "And God raised us up with Christ and seated us with him in the heavenly realms in Christ Jesus." Spiritually speaking, in Jesus, we're above the smog. So the next time you're choking on the heavy atmosphere around you, pray, "Take me up, Lord!" and then thank Him when He answers.

The atmosphere around me gets so heavy, Lord. Lift me up above the smog of this life. Remind me that my spirit already resides with You! Amen.

Jesus over All

A cord of three strands is not quickly broken.

Two young women were overheard daydreaming about their future spouses. "What sort of man do you want to marry?" asked the first young woman. "Someone who will put me first," answered the second. "I want to know I'm the first thing on his mind when he wakes up and the last thing he thinks of when he falls asleep."

Many people would agree, but they're actually mistaken. Finding a spouse who will put you above all else could be disastrous. Why? Because every truly successful marriage involves *three* beings: husband, wife, and God. There's simply no way to do marriage as God designed it while leaving Him out of it. But it doesn't stop there: God must be at the center, the most beloved One of all.

If you've been asking the Lord to send you a spouse, pray for a partner who'll love God more than he or she loves you. It will make all the difference.

Send me a spouse who loves You even more than he/she loves me, Lord. I know that then we'll truly be equipped for life and marriage. Amen.

Moody? Or Steadfast?

Out of the same mouth come praise and cursing. My brothers and sisters, this should not be.

James 3:10

According to *Merriam-Webster*, a *mood* is "a conscious state of mind or predominant emotion."[5] But that "state of mind" or "emotion" can change in a heartbeat. For some, Christianity is merely a mood. Their actions are generally Christlike because their state of mind and emotions are positive—for the moment—but that could change very quickly.

In today's verse, James warned his listeners against praising and cursing out of the same mouth. It's possible to do this through our words, but also in our hearts, without ever saying a word. One minute we're deliriously in love with Jesus; the next minute He's asking a little too much of us, and then suddenly He doesn't look so good anymore.

Is your faith moody and fickle? Remember that the steadfast believer isn't the one who floats around on a cloud all day; she's the one whose love for God is contingent on *His* steadfastness, not *her* current state of mind.

Lord, forgive me if I've been moody and fickle in my love for You. Make my faith in You unwavering and steadfast. Amen.

Displacement

Guard your heart above all else, for it is the source of life.

Proverbs 4:23 HCSB

isplacement is a term often used in physics and engineering. The easiest way to illustrate displacement is by filling a jar first with water, then with marbles, one by one. Each marble will occupy the volume that would otherwise have been occupied by the water, and soon water will spill over the rim.

Like marbles in a jar of water, certain emotions and thoughts will displace the goodness in a person's heart. The redeemed human heart has an astonishing capacity for love, but hatred (or its cousins, such as unforgiveness, jealousy, self-pity, and pride) is deadly. Nurse a grudge, and bitterness will displace love. The good news is that the opposite is also true: the love of God in a Christian's heart will displace all that's dark.

If you're struggling with sinful emotions, open yourself up more fully to the love of God until it occupies every corner of your heart.

Displace my wrong thoughts and feelings with purity, honesty, humility, and love, Lord. Amen.

Within Reach

I was shown mercy so that in me, the worst of sinners, Christ Jesus might display his immense patience.

Many pastors and other church leaders struggle with feeling as though they can't be themselves in public because others see them as spiritually superior—simply because of their position. In fact, many people believe that church leaders enjoy a relationship with God they themselves could never achieve. After all, God loves preachers more than He loves regular people, right?

Wrong.

No one has any more access to God than you do! The same saint—Paul—who was "caught up to paradise and heard inexpressible things" (2 Corinthians 12:4) also called himself the worst of sinners (1 Timothy 1:15). You, too, can have as much God as you want. Resist the notion that only leaders can truly win God's love and favor. The deep things of God are within reach of every Christian, including you. He's your Teacher and Guide, the Revealer of Truth, who loves and delights in you. You just need to be willing to go where He leads.

Lord, I thank You for loving me just as much as You love all Your other children. With You, there are no favorites. Amen.

Loving Intervention

As a father has compassion on his children, so the LORD has compassion on those who fear him.

Psalm 103:13

As a young father helps his eight-year-old with her first woodworking project, he knows he'll have to sneak a few extra nails into the project to stabilize it, but he doesn't mind. Meanwhile, the man's wife quietly refolds the T-shirts their son folded while trying to do his household chores. This is what we do for the ones we love; we quietly intervene when their efforts are clumsy or unskilled, especially when their hearts are in the right place.

Yet we struggle to believe that God would do the same for us. Instead, we wallow in self-condemnation because we can't do everything flawlessly. The more perfectionistic we are, the harder it is to believe God will bless and love us. Yes, we should always do our best, but we can trust Him to "add a few extra nails" while we're not looking. He isn't surprised by our imperfections, and He doesn't love us any less because of them.

Thank You so much, Lord, for picking up the slack when I make mistakes, and for loving me all the while. Amen.

The Bottomless Tank

*I pray that you . . . know this love that surpasses knowledge—that
you may be filled to the measure of all the fullness of God.*

Ephesians 3:17–19

At 55 million square feet of space, SubTropolis is a man-made cave high in the bluffs above the Missouri River in Kansas City, Missouri, that houses more than 55 businesses and provides over 2,000 jobs.[6] Reputedly the largest underground storage facility in the world, even this immense cave could not begin to hold the love of God—assuming, of course, that His love could be contained. God's love is uncontainable, immeasurable, and limitless. It also cannot be earned.

God loves you—today, right this moment, for exactly who you are, how you are, and where you are—no more and no less than He would love you if you were to do a 180-degree change. That's because His love is not determined by worldly measurements; He loves you because of who *He* is. And no storage space, not even the universe itself, can contain, measure, or limit Him.

*Help me, Lord, to grasp the magnitude of Your love for me—especially
when I am feeling unloved, unlovely, and unlovable. Amen.*

Body Language

I will praise you as long as I live, and in your name I will lift up my hands.

Psalm 63:4

f you gently lift a skittish dog's tail as he walks, he'll gain confidence. Why? Because a confident dog never tucks his tail. In other words, when a dog feels a certain way, he adopts a certain body language. The opposite is also true: if you position your dog a certain way, his feelings will often follow suit. This confirms what psychologists have long known—body language is powerful. It not only reveals what we're feeling; it can *change* what we're feeling.

The next time the heavens are silent and you're having a difficult time connecting with God, try this: lift your hands as you pray. Don't be timid—spread your hands wide and lift your face as though you're expecting to receive a deluge of blessing. Get into a posture to receive, and your emotions will fall into place. The end result is that you'll become far more receptive to the love and presence of God.

Lord, right now, I lift my hands and my face to You. I receive Your affection, Your approval, Your love. Amen.

Faith and Doubt

I keep my eyes always on the LORD. . . . I will not be shaken.

Psalm 16:8

What's the number one way a person can express his or her love for God? Many would say, "By having faith!" Then why do we so often fail? In Mark 9, a man's son was healed by Jesus. At one point, Jesus gently rebuked the father for doubting Him, and the man responded, "I do believe; help me overcome my unbelief!" (v. 24). Can you relate? *I believe—and yet I have doubts! But, Lord, I want to be free of these doubts. Help!*

All Christians have moments of uncertainty, but consistent unbelief is damaging to a person's relationship with God. Are you a believer who doesn't believe? Do you want to be free of doubts and instead live up to the name "Believer"? Turn to God and ask Him to help you bank everything on Jesus, to trust that He died and rose again, and to believe that His love is *enough*. God asks for our faith, and then Jesus makes it perfect (Hebrews 12:2).

I want so much to love You by always trusting You, Lord. Please help me overcome my unbelief. Amen.

Crucial Questions

Do not be misled: "Bad company corrupts good character."

1 Corinthians 15:33

Some relationships are so unhealthy that anyone can spot the problems. If a man ridicules his fiancée for her faith, isolates her from her family, and throws a jealous fit if she so much as speaks to a male coworker, it's obvious she needs to end the relationship immediately. But what if the warning signs are more subtle? If you have occasional "red flags" about a love interest (or even a friendship), how can you know if you're being too cautious or if you should run in the other direction? Ask yourself the following questions:

- *Are we adding to each other's lives, or subtracting?*
- *Does he/she draw me closer to God, further from Him, or neither?*
- *Does the relationship stir up anger, fear, or insecurity?*
- *How would I feel if Jesus accompanied me on my next outing with this person?*
- *Is the relationship directed by the Spirit of God and His truth?*

How did you do?

Father, give me the courage to take a close, honest look at my relationships and make any changes You'd like me to make. Amen.

Filling Our Love Tanks

Dear friends, since God so loved us, we also ought to love one another.

1 John 4:11

Some snake species regularly go without food for six months—but a tarantula can survive for more than two years! When the heat rises to more than 110 degrees, camels can live for five days without water—and during the winter months they can survive for half a year.

Humans aren't as resilient. We'll survive only a few weeks without food and a few days without water. But we need love daily. Thankfully, God is never absent. A spouse might die; children might move away; friends might be in short supply. But God is the Friend, the Lover, the Brother whose love is always accessible. To keep our "love tanks" full, we must learn to tap quickly into the love of God.

Let's also remember that the people around us crave love just as much as we do, but some aren't plugged in to the Source. So receive God's love daily, but also give it daily.

I'm so grateful, Lord, that You created me to need love every day and then made sure I can always receive that love from You. Amen.

SEPTEMBER

Give thanks to the LORD, for he is
good; his love endures forever.

1 Chronicles 16:34

Love and Thornbushes

"Therefore I will block her path with thornbushes; I will wall her in so that she cannot find her way."

This verse was written in response to Israel's unfaithfulness to God. Because He loved His people so much, He decided to hedge them in so they wouldn't destroy themselves by chasing after other gods. At first glance, it might sound harsh to block someone's path with thorns, to ensure she can't find her way. But the Lord's motivation was intense love.

Has the Lord ever blocked your path? Sometimes He'll use circumstances to lead you to a place you'd rather not be so you'll turn back to Him, or so you'll stop a certain behavior that's damaging you. Maybe you've spent a great deal of time and energy chasing after a particular job or relationship, but you feel as if you're banging your head against a wall. Is it possible that God has erected that wall because of His commitment to you? If so, thank Him for blocking your path, and seek His will for you.

Lord, I know sometimes You put thornbushes in my path because You love me. Help me to find the path You have created for me. Amen.

Love and Conversation

Never stop praying.

1 Thessalonians 5:17 NLT

You have lunch with your brother every Saturday because you can't imagine doing life without his insight.

You're so comfortable with your best friend that shallow small talk is completely unnecessary.

When you call your college roommate, the two of you pick up the conversation right where you left off six months earlier.

When we talk with a dearly loved friend, we're completely comfortable. We give lots of feedback and expect it in return. Sadly, however, when we pray, we sometimes feel tongue-tied or clumsy, and we don't really even expect an answer. We don't fully realize we can converse with our Creator, and that He's not only capable of answering but *eager* to answer.

So what's the solution? To be persistent. To practice communing with God until it's second nature. To return again and again to prayer until we're just as able to stop and chat with our heavenly Best Friend as we are with our earthly one.

Lord, thank You for wanting to talk to me, anytime and anywhere, about anything. I'm so grateful for Your listening ear. Amen.

Created to Love God

"Bring . . . everyone who is called by my name, whom I created for my glory, whom I formed and made."

Isaiah 43:6–7

When it's time to migrate, salmon will do whatever it takes to get from Point A to Point B. One particular salmon was tagged before migrating across Alaska. Scientists discovered she traveled more than thirty miles each day, for a total of two thousand miles in two months—without ever eating![1]

Animals migrate. Tides rise and fall. Planets orbit. These things happen because God decided that each piece of His creation would fulfill a certain purpose. People were created with the purpose of knowing and loving God. Caribou will migrate across impossible barriers, and trees will grow right through fences because they were created to do so, yet we humans will resist God. We're the only living things that defy our highest purpose! The result is that we're miserable until we do what we were meant to do.

If you're feeling restless and unhappy, maybe you've been avoiding your highest calling. Turn to God, and find your purpose.

I'm miserable whenever I stray from You, Lord. I make a fresh commitment to You to fulfill my highest calling: loving You. Amen.

Communicate Love

David was dancing before the LORD with all his might, while he and all Israel were bringing up the ark of the LORD with shouts and the sound of trumpets.

2 Samuel 6:14–15

Poor communication is destructive to any relationship. Because of the nature of the marriage relationship, however, it's most destructive—besides being irritating and frustrating—when it occurs between spouses. "Talk to me!" a spouse pleads, only to see the other spouse walk away.

Are we guilty of walking away from God? Although God has created billions of people, He longs for a personal relationship with each one of us. How can we communicate with One we cannot see? First, we can talk to Him in prayer. And, second, we can worship Him. When David and the Israelites returned the ark of the covenant to Jerusalem, they rejoiced mightily to the sound of trumpets and shouting. And David, the king of all Israel, led the way, dancing, leaping, and jumping in a most undignified way. Imagine God laughing and clapping to see the earthly king worshiping the heavenly King with such love and enthusiasm!

How amazing, Lord, that You want a personal relationship with me! Teach me how to communicate my love for You both to You and to others. Amen.

The God Who Always Shows Up

From the ends of the earth I call to you. . . . For you have been my refuge.

Psalm 61:2–3

In October 2017, the *Mercury News* shared a video of a lone postal truck driving down the streets of a Santa Rosa neighborhood. The thing that made this familiar sight so bizarre was that most of the houses had been destroyed by wildfires.[2] The scene brings to mind the proverb that "neither snow nor rain nor heat nor gloom of night" will stop the mail. Come what may—including disaster, it seems—we can always know the postal carrier will show up.

No one, however, is more reliable than our loving Father. Granted, many Christians have experienced dry seasons, when it felt as if God were playing hide-and-seek. But He *always* shows up when we call. If you read David's most anguished psalms, you see that even as he begged God to come to his aid, he invariably circled back around to the fact that God never, ever failed him in the end. He won't fail you either.

I trust in Your love, Lord. I know You will always come when I call; You'll never fail to show up. Amen.

A Secure Future

*You created my inmost being; you knit me together in my mother's
womb.*

Psalm 139:13

When a new baby comes into a home, there are usually at
least a few conversations regarding the tiny person's future:

"Oh, I just know she'll be a doctor, like me," says New
Mommy.

"But first she'll go to my alma mater!" declares New Daddy.

"Maybe she'll get married when she graduates and have
four grandbabies for us!"

"No, she'll be a professor . . ."

Why do family and friends feel they must map out a little
one's future almost twenty years early? Because they want the
future of the child they love to be prosperous and secure.

Our heavenly Father, who loves us with an unfathomable
love, also wants our lives to be safe, secure, and filled with
hope. Consequently, He has plans for each of us even before
we're "knit together" in our mothers' wombs. Everything God
does, He does out of love. So we'd be wise to seek His will in
everything we do.

*Thank You, Father, for Your great love. Help me to seek Your will
for each step of my life, knowing Your answers will be the best ones
for me. Amen.*

Loving the Wounded

Live as children of light.

Ephesians 5:8

Shrapnel consists of tiny chunks of material such as metal. When an explosive is detonated, shrapnel can fly through the air at tremendous speed, causing horrific damage to bystanders.

When someone we know is facing a crisis, we offer that person our prayers, help with errands, or give other types of assistance. These are wonderful and necessary gestures, but, far too often, we forget that every crisis causes shrapnel. Sometimes the people closest to the one suffering are doing a great deal of suffering themselves. Don't overlook them. When a friend is recovering from an accident, acknowledge the vital role that his caretaker plays. When someone loses a husband, offer a listening ear to not just the widow but the children as well. In this way, you'll be shining God's love and light into the dark corners where those who suffer are often overlooked.

Lord, is there someone in my life who's been wounded by the shrapnel of a difficult situation? Please show me creative ways to make his or her life easier. Amen.

Little Paper Blessings

May the LORD bless you and protect you.

Have you ever wished you could give someone an extra-special and personal blessing for his or her birthday? Try this idea:

E-mail as many of the birthday boy's or girl's friends and family members as possible. Ask them to send you two or three written blessings—a memory, a word of encouragement, or a description of what they love and appreciate about the person who's being celebrated. Ask everyone to be specific. For example, "You're a great person" is fine, but this is even better: "I've never heard you say a harsh word about anyone. Thank you for inspiring me to speak kindly of others." Then print out all the blessings, cut them into strips, and put them all into a decorative jar.

All you need to pull this gift together is a little time, a cute jar, and a list of e-mail addresses. With any luck, your friend will end up with enough blessings to read one every week for a year!

Lord, help me never to forget the power of blessing others with my words. Amen.

Strength to Persevere

Let us run with perseverance the race marked out for us.

Hebrews 12:1

Monarch butterflies perform phenomenal feats of perseverance every year as they migrate some three thousand miles—farther than any other butterfly. In September and October, they begin their flights south, doggedly battling winds and storms and other obstacles until they reach their destinations. Then, in spring, they start the return trip, which will take them until summer. No one butterfly makes the entire round trip; it takes at least four generations of monarchs to complete the cycle, which could be called the world's most incredible relay race. What determination! What perseverance! What commitment!

The perseverance of the monarch is the kind of perseverance the Bible calls on us to have in our daily lives. In all the trials and tribulations of living, we are to stand firm and keep the faith, knowing that the love of our heavenly Father will help us through every storm.

Father God, grant me the courage and strength to persevere, trusting Your love to help me stand firm in every trial. Amen.

Love in the Details

"Are not five sparrows sold for two pennies? Yet not one of them is forgotten by God."

Luke 12:6

You've created a video you're proud of. The content is great, and you've uploaded it to YouTube. But then you hit a snag. Your clever custom thumbnail won't save. You feel frustrated, and part of you wants to pray and ask the Lord to fix the problem or show you a solution, but you feel silly thinking such a thing.

It's not at *all* silly to take even the least of your troubles to the Lord. If you're tempted to say, "He's got enough to take care of without my petty concerns," consider that there are two major flaws with this statement: first, it's impossible for a God who's omnipotent to have too much on His plate, and second, if the Lord cares about the welfare of tiny sparrows, He certainly cares about the details of your life. It's impossible for Him to be too involved! And rest assured He's pleased when you include Him in every aspect of life.

Lord, I'm astonished by how big Your love is. Thank You for caring about even the least of my troubles. Amen.

Remember

"Look here. I have made you a part of Me, written you on the palms of My hands."

Many people go to great lengths to commemorate September 11, 2001. But other people believe it's time to stop focusing so intently on that heartbreaking day. Both viewpoints are understandable. Sometimes we have to guard against getting trapped in our grief because life does go on after a tragedy. On the other hand, nearly three thousand people died in the attack, meaning that countless Americans lost loved ones that day.

When we lose someone we love, we can continue to live *while also remembering.* Grief is not something that magically ends one day. We're forever changed by those we've loved and then lost, whether a spouse, a parent or grandparent, a miscarried child, or a dear friend. Once we've loved someone, that person is forever engraved on our hearts—as we are forever engraved on the heart of God. It's good to remember.

Comfort all the Americans who lost someone on this day, Lord. May we not take our friends and families for granted. Amen.

You Can Still Forgive

Forgive one another if any of you has a grievance against someone.
Forgive as the Lord forgave you.

Colossians 3:13

When you consider who you might need to forgive, does the Lord bring anyone to mind? Maybe you truly want to forgive so your heart can be at peace—but what if the person has already passed away or will not have a relationship with you?

Some things require give-and-take. For example, you can't have a conversation with someone unless he or she takes an active role. Otherwise, you're just talking to yourself. But have you ever dressed a baby who's sleeping so deeply she doesn't even wake up? You don't need her participation. Even though it might be slightly awkward, dressing a sleeping child is entirely possible. So it is with forgiveness: active participation from the other person is great, but definitely not necessary. You can still do your part. The person you need to forgive doesn't have to *accept* your forgiveness; you only have to *extend* it. This is love in action, and it'll bring freedom and peace.

Thank You, Lord, for setting my heart free right now as I choose to forgive _____ once and for all. Amen.

Be Firm

Do not move an ancient boundary stone set up by your ancestors.

Proverbs 22:28

You've just moved into a new apartment and can't wait to start decorating. But then your friend stops by and immediately starts scurrying from room to room: "Teal would look amazing in here!" she calls out. "And these windows are just begging for Roman shades. Let's get to the department store right now—I'll drive!"

Chances are, your friend's motives are harmless, yet she's clearly stomping all over your domain. You have several choices: you can do nothing and end up with a decor you don't like; you can shout, "Get out of my house!" and destroy the friendship; or you can do the loving thing and reestablish your boundaries.

Love and firmness are *not* mutually exclusive. When someone tries to take control where that person doesn't belong, say something like, "No, I appreciate your ideas, but . . ." or, "Thanks, I've got this." Be loving, but be resolute.

Sometimes I'm not good at maintaining boundaries, Lord. Give me the resolve and boldness to be lovingly firm. Amen.

Be Present

We . . . desire to live honorably in every way.

Hebrews 13:18

One of the easiest but most neglected ways to love and honor someone is by simply being present. Experts say that the average adult today checks his phone more than a hundred times per day.[3] Sometimes all it takes is one intriguing e-mail, Instagram, or Facebook post to tie up forty-five minutes when all you meant to do was take a quick glance.

One of the most tragic results of this distraction in our lives is that our relationships are being profoundly affected. Being in the same room with a friend or family member isn't equal to being *with* him or her. You might think you're barely peeking at your phone, but that person you supposedly care about is acutely aware that you're not really there.

Today, consider your phone off-limits, especially while interacting with other people. Not only will they feel more valued; you might enjoy the most stress-free day you've had in weeks.

Lord, help me to be present in my relationships with the priceless people around me by maintaining distance from my gadgets. Amen.

Loving by Remembering

When your words came, I ate them; they were my joy and my heart's delight.

According to Learning-Mind.com, an unborn baby can remember certain sounds just twenty weeks after conception. Winston Churchill could recite almost every Shakespearean play. And Arturo Toscanini, a conductor from Italy, could remember every note from four hundred different musical compositions![4]

Do you realize that remembering can be an indicator of love? Think about it: the last time someone remembered your birthday or gave you a gift that was very specific to your personality, you probably blurted out, "You remembered!" because you felt loved and valued. One way to love God well is to remember as much about Him as you can. The simplest way to do this is to commit His Word to memory. Consider downloading an app that narrates the Bible and setting a favorite chapter on loop. Before you know it, you'll be reciting verse after verse. Imagine God's delight as you tell others about Him by calling to mind His own words. Perhaps He'll say, "She remembered!"

I want to learn and then remember as much as I can about who You are, Lord. Strengthen my memory for Your purposes. Amen.

Communication and Trust

Since they were unable to communicate, they stopped working on the city and went their separate ways.

Genesis 11:8 THE VOICE

Have you ever tried to initiate an important conversation with a loved one only to have him clam up? Learn to cultivate an atmosphere of love and trust when it comes to communication. This might require breaking some old habits that tend to shut people down.

1. *Watch out for gestures and other body language that convey shame.* Shaking your head, rolling your eyes—these things will quickly bring a conversation to a halt.
2. *No meltdowns.* If the other person says something upsetting, try to keep your composure and talk it out calmly. This way, you'll be approachable even when others make mistakes.
3. *Make room for feelings.* If someone expresses emotions that aren't pretty, such as anger, jealousy, or depression, don't shy away. Let the person know that certain behaviors might be unacceptable, but feelings are okay.

Follow these guidelines, and watch your friends and family members open up to you more and more.

Guard my mouth, Lord, and help me to break any harmful communication habits so that others will open up to me. Amen.

Loving in Anomalies, Part 1

Rejoice in all the good things the LORD your God has given you.
Deuteronomy 26:11 CSB

Although they're in the Arctic Circle, the Lofoten Islands of Norway have a temperate climate thanks to the Gulf Stream. They also boast massive mountains, fascinating fjords, and breathtaking beauty. When God created this wonderland amidst the frozen, barren Arctic, what might He have been thinking? Was His goal to form an oasis of beauty to show the people His majesty? Did He hope the grandeur of His creation might prompt people to stand in awe of Him, to seek Him, to love Him?

The unusual climate in these picturesque islands is what science calls an *anomaly*, something far different from what we would expect. But our God, who is the Giver of all good things, has created it as one more demonstration of His love. Today, look around you. Can you even begin to name every single gift from God that's in your line of sight? What love!

Lord, everything You give us is good. Thank You for Your love-drenched blessings! Amen.

Loving in Anomalies, Part 2

Some of them saw Him walking on the surface of the water.

Mark 6:49 THE VOICE

Have you ever heard someone say that God *cannot* do anything contrary to the laws of science? If this were true, how could Jesus have walked on water?

One of the many things God has done out of His bottomless love for us is to establish the system of rules, which we know as scientific laws. Because of these laws, we can live in the assurance that spring will follow winter, we won't fall off the face of the earth, water will turn to ice at the right temperature, and the planets won't go helter-skelter and smash into each other in a celestial traffic jam.

But God is always at the controls of the system. And He has His eye on each and every one of us. So if we need Him, He'll come quickly, perhaps even breaking the scientific laws He created . . . perhaps even by walking on the water.

Father, how amazing it is that even the laws of science must bow down to You. And how amazing that One who creates those laws would willingly break them to rescue me. Amen.

Do-Nothing Day

Jesus said, "Let's go off by ourselves to a quiet place and rest awhile."

Mark 6:31 NLT

God loves us so much that He invented rest and recreation. History shows that people have engaged in games, picnics, and other leisurely activities from the beginning. Modern society, however, moves far too quickly. All day, every day, it's *go-go-go-go-go-go*. More than ever, we're feeling the stress of overbooked schedules.

Why not say yes to God's loving gifts of rest and leisure by allowing yourself to slow *way* down once in a while? Schedule a Do-Nothing Day. When that day arrives, settle into a hammock with a book and stay there until the sun sets. Indulge in a craft you used to enjoy. Spend the whole day in your pajamas. Or eat pizza with extra cheese . . . in bed.

Does this sound a bit radical? Remember, the worst that can happen is a few crumbs in your sheets. God loved you enough to invent rest; thank Him by enjoying His invention.

Lord, have I allowed my schedule to get too overloaded? Please help me make time to enjoy Your gifts of rest and leisure. Amen.

The Relationship Sinkhole

He lifted me out of the slimy pit, out of the mud and mire; he set my feet on a rock and gave me a firm place to stand.

Psalm 40:2

Imagine looking out your window at your quiet, comfortable neighborhood when the house across the street suddenly starts collapsing and crumbling into the earth. That's what happened one July day in Land O'Lakes, Florida, thanks to a sinkhole that sent residents scurrying for safety. What started as a depression the size of a small pool quickly developed into a hole 260 feet wide and 50 feet deep that swallowed two homes.[5] Imagine how those homeowners felt later, knowing they'd been carrying out their daily lives on top of something so treacherous.

Unforgiveness is much like a sinkhole: deadly, unseen, unpredictable, and threatening to destroy relationships. Is there someone you need to forgive? Or an offense you need to take to the cross? Do so quickly. Relationships can't handle the weight of bitterness; sooner or later, everything will come crashing down. Allow God's love and forgiveness toward you to heal every wound so that your relationships can thrive.

Lord, I take hold of Your grace to help me forgive every offense so my relationships can be built on solid ground. Amen.

Love Magnet

Do you show contempt for the riches of his kindness . . . not realizing that God's kindness is intended to lead you to repentance?

Have you ever used a magnetic sweeper? Consisting of a long, magnetic strip on wheels connected to a handle, this tool is fabulous for picking up sharp, metal debris after a construction project. Just roll it through the grass and it'll pull up countless tiny, hidden fragments. Sometimes it'll even extricate something that's been hiding for years, just waiting to cause a flat tire. More than one person has discovered a decades-old, rusty washer or small tool.

Love, too, has a way of pulling unseen and potentially dangerous nuisances to the surface and into the light, even when they've been there for decades. How many times has a buried hang-up or wound caused pain and damage even though it seemed trivial? God's love and kindness will draw out those issues and lead us to repentance. Similarly, when we show consistent loving-kindness to someone else, he or she is far more likely to open up about past hurts and sins.

I choose to open my heart to You, Lord, and allow You to pull to the surface all the hidden debris that keeps me from loving You completely. Amen.

Fun in the Sun

The streets of the city shall be full of boys and girls playing in its streets.

Zechariah 8:5 ESV

Tag. Red Rover. Kick the Can. Is this how you spent your days as a child? If not, your parents can probably tell you all about games like these. Relatively few years have passed since kids ran themselves silly in backyards nearly every day. Today, many children are missing out on the bliss of playing in the sun—but so are many adults!

Your loving Father designed you to flourish mentally, physically, and spiritually through time spent outdoors. Take care of *you* by tapping into your inner child. Outdoor play is invigorating, healthy, and inexpensive—and it's not just for kids. Pick up some gently used Rollerblades at the thrift store and spend the day learning (or relearning) how to use them. Or put on some comfortable shoes and take a walk with a friend. Some fun in the sun will quickly set all things right again.

Thank You so much, Lord, for fields, trees, sunshine, and backyards. Help me to find new ways to enjoy Your beautiful world. Amen.

Dealing with Frustration?

Fools give full vent to their rage, but the wise bring calm in the end.

Proverbs 29:11

Eight-year-old Justin was thirsty. As he reached toward the counter for his juice, his sleeve caught the coffee canister, and three pounds of coffee grains cascaded all over the kitchen floor. Mom gasped but bit her tongue just in time. "Wow," she said calmly. "That's quite a mess! Why don't you go get the broom? I'll get the vacuum, and we'll clean this up together."

Justin was fortunate to have a parent who knew how to deal lovingly and calmly with frustration. How often do you give in to the urge to roll your eyes, nag, or speak harshly when others frustrate you? Try not to let your emotions take the lead, causing unnecessary strife and even heaping shame on the people around you. Instead, remember that they're flawed (just as you are), and that handling frustrations with grace and composure is one of the most loving things you can do—and it's what God does for you.

Thank You for the virtue of self-control, Lord, that allows me to deal with my frustrations in a godly, rather than an immature, way. Amen.

All of You for All of Him

Jesus . . . became to us wisdom from God, righteousness and sanctification and redemption . . . "Let the one who boasts, boast in the Lord."

1 Corinthians 1:30–31 ESV

In His profound love, Jesus offers us a trade through salvation: all of us for all of Him. He gets all our garbage—our sin, compulsions, horrible thoughts, and twisted motives. We get all His righteousness. And we reflect His righteousness as we perform acts of service to others in His name. Every time we help someone else, we show the love of Christ.

Because we give the Lord all our junk, and He does not condemn us, we have no reason to condemn ourselves. But we have no reason to boast of our service to Him either. After all, the love we give others is so small compared to the unending love He gives us. We can only say with Paul, "By the grace of God I am what I am" (1 Corinthians 15:10). A beloved child of the King.

Lord, along with Paul, I'll boast in You, not in myself. Thank You for saving all of me and giving me all of You. Amen.

Not What They Seem

Fools find no pleasure in understanding but delight in airing their own opinions.

If you're not familiar with culinary terms, when you hear the word *sweetbread*, you might picture something like cinnamon toast. Actually, sweetbread is neither sweet nor bread—it's the thymus or pancreas from a lamb or calf. Or imagine you were new to the English language and heard someone mention a prairie dog. You'd be more likely to picture a creature that barks and wags its tail than a rodent, wouldn't you? Things are not always what they seem!

The same is true of people. Sometimes we hear one or two so-called facts about a person, and we hastily form an opinion that's way off the mark. Loving one's neighbor, however, means shelving our opinion until we truly get to know a person. Imagine how much better we'd get along with others if we put aside all those rumors we've heard from "reliable" sources. Today, practice goodwill by remembering that things—and people—aren't always what they seem.

Lord, help me remember that everyone I meet deserves to start with a clean slate. Forgive me for making hasty and uninformed judgments. Amen.

Loving Through Encouragement

So then, let us . . . build each other up.

Romans 14:19 NLT

To encourage someone is to build up his or her confidence—not through flattery but through genuine support. All people need to be affirmed and encouraged. Think of the new employee who beams when the boss praises her contribution to an important project. Or the grandpa who stands taller when his wife thanks him for being so great with the grandkids. This is the way God wired His children. The need for encouragement and affirmation lies deep within the soul of all people—no matter what age they are.

When's the last time you intentionally offered affirmation to someone who needed a pick-me-up? One of the surest ways to love a person is to say, through words or actions, "I believe in you." We can bring healing, strength, and support to others by cheering them on, reminding them of the reasons we admire them, and calling forth the champion that lives in every human heart.

Teach me, Lord, to see the best qualities in the people in my life and then to affirm and encourage them. Amen.

A Quick Response

"Whether you turn to the right or to the left, your ears will hear a voice behind you, saying, 'This is the way; walk in it.'"

Isaiah 30:21

She was sixteen, with a brand-new driver's license, and thrilled to be driving herself to school. As she began to back down the driveway, she didn't see the wagon her brother had left behind her car. Suddenly she heard her mother yell, "Stop!" and hit the brakes. Her quick response probably saved her parents a big repair bill.

Sometimes, if we're about to make a bad choice, God will lovingly protect us by calling out, "Stop!" Our quick response could keep us from heartache or disaster. Imagine you're about to confide in a colleague about a personal problem, only to feel a hesitation in your heart. Even if you don't understand why, listen to the Lord's warning and resist the urge to charge ahead. Talk it over with Him later, and you'll probably realize He kept you from making a painful mistake.

Listen for God's voice, and determine to obey quickly, knowing He loves you and works to protect you.

Teach me to be the kind of child who responds immediately to Your voice of protection, Lord. Amen.

Here Comes the Sun

Be joyful in hope, patient in affliction, faithful in prayer.

Romans 12:12

In many parts of the country, autumn is that time of year when temperatures can change by forty degrees or more between sunup and midafternoon. You go to work in a coat, fuzzy boots, and scarf, but when you leave for lunch, you immediately start peeling off layers. In the fall, the absence of the sun's warmth at six in the morning is very noticeable, but so is its presence a few hours later, so dressing appropriately can be a challenge. Even the frostiest morning can turn into a sunny, gorgeous day.

If you're in a cold, dark period of life, know that things can shift drastically—and very quickly. Hold on to hope and to the knowledge that God's love never fades. Cling to Him in the darkness, and rest assured that the sun *will* reappear soon. You might not see it at the moment, but it hasn't gone anywhere, and neither has your Father.

I cling to hope, Lord, and to the assurance that You love me more than I can understand. Please quickly chase the darkness away with the warmth of Your light. Amen.

Tackle or Pardon?

The words of the wise bring healing.

Proverbs 12:18 NLT

When told to choose their battles, some people might say, "I'm not sure how to differentiate between a battle that's worth confronting and one that should be quickly pardoned." What should you do when the line seems vague?

First, ask yourself three questions. For example, perhaps your teenage son can be hot-tempered at times, so ask yourself:

- *How often?* (Frequently? Or rarely?)
- *Across how many situations?* (At the slightest provocation? Or when burning the candle at both ends?)
- *With what intensity?* (Stomping around in the backyard, or putting his fist through a wall?)

Now that you have a clearer picture of what's happening, you can choose how to best handle it. Whether you decide an issue needs to be tackled or pardoned, remember that both can be carried out in a loving way. And deciding that a battle must be dealt with doesn't leave out love. In fact, sometimes it's the most loving thing you can do.

Lord, give me lots of wisdom as I figure out which conflicts are worth tackling and which should be overlooked. Amen.

Catch the Foxes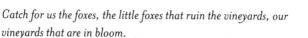

Catch for us the foxes, the little foxes that ruin the vineyards, our vineyards that are in bloom.

Song of Songs 2:15

Foxes have a reputation for being cunning and agile. They're also elusive. Although they live in cities and towns as well as forests, we don't often see them. When they're not raising their young, they live alone rather than in packs, and they do most of their hunting after dark. Foxes have excellent night vision and tend to hunt in a way that's similar to cats—ambushing and pouncing. Some can even climb trees!

In this verse from Song of Solomon, the lover and the beloved are told by their friends to "catch the foxes," that is, the things that distract and steal from a loving relationship. Even a relationship with God that's consistently fruitful, like a vineyard in bloom, can be threatened. Believers must be diligent to spot potential "foxes," which are elusive and sneaky, and quickly do away with them.

Are there foxes in your spiritual vineyard? Don't try to domesticate them. Get rid of them *now*.

Lord, may I never try to make a pet out of a fox that's threatening to damage my friendship with You. Amen.

OCTOBER

....

For in Christ Jesus neither circumcision nor
uncircumcision has any value. The only thing that
counts is faith expressing itself through love.

Galatians 5:6

Solid Rock

*The Sovereign L*ORD *is my strength; he makes my feet like the feet of
a deer, he enables me to tread on the heights.*

Habakkuk 3:19

Have you ever seen a nature film in which antelope or mountain goats are running nimbly over the rocky sides of steep mountains, seemingly oblivious to the imminent danger? With every step it seems the animals should go tumbling down the side of the mountain. We marvel at the agility, strength, and courage of even the youngest ones!

In today's verse, Habakkuk praised God for His protection, even as He allowed him to leap from one potentially dangerous situation to another. As we step toward certain peril (and perhaps especially when we're oblivious to the evils and dangers around us), God takes our feet and plants them on the solid rock. Occasionally, He might allow us to miss our footing, to teach us that we need to depend on Him and look to Him for guidance. But when we've learned the lesson, He again places us on a secure landing. He doesn't let His children fall!

*Lord, teach me to always look to You for guidance and direction.
Keep my feet on the solid Rock of Jesus. Amen.*

There's a Better Way

"I needed clothes and you clothed me, I was sick and you looked after me, I was in prison and you came to visit me."

Matthew 25:36

For the first time, Amy had joined a few members of her church for an afternoon of prison ministry. As the inmates filed in, Amy smiled as her brother, Hank, greeted each one by name. She was taken aback, however, when Hank went out of his way to start a friendly conversation with a man who'd committed an especially heinous crime. She couldn't understand how Hank could show such kindness to someone like that.

Are there certain members of society who don't deserve our compassion? Jesus didn't seem to think so. He taught that *all* people need to know there's a way to live that's powerful, fulfilling, and pure. If we don't show those who know only violence and depravity that God offers a better way, who will? Some people will never get a taste of God's love unless they experience it in our words and actions. Will you be a messenger of His love?

Lord, I don't want to make it easy for anyone to say, "No one ever showed me God's better way." Help me to have compassion on all people. Amen.

# Open Arms

"For this son of mine was dead and is alive again; he was lost and is found."

The girl adjusted the straps of her backpack and wearily moved on. She had run away from home months before, believing she'd find fun and easy living on the streets. However, it didn't take long to discover that her home hadn't been the miserable prison she'd thought it was, and she longed to be back with her family. Overcome with regret, she trudged toward home. But looming in her thoughts was the question, *How will my family receive me?*

In Luke, Jesus told the story of the prodigal son. The young man had left home, squandered all his money, and was starving when he decided to go home. Imagine his amazement when his father received him with open arms!

The father in Jesus' parable represents our Father, God. The son is any one of us. When we sin, all God asks is that we turn back to Him. When we seek His forgiveness, He promises to forgive.

Dear Father, thank You for loving me so much that You're always ready to receive me back and forgive me. Help me not to wander away from You. Amen.

The Enemy of Self-Awareness

*I want to be found belonging to Him, not clinging to my own
righteousness . . . but actively relying on the faithfulness of the
Anointed One.*

Philippians 3:9 THE VOICE

*L*ook at everyone nodding their heads and sitting on the edge of their seats. I'm
rockin' it this morning. I just get better and better at leading Sunday school!

*Everyone's awfully quiet. I must be making a mess of this Bible study. No one
wants to hear what I have to say.*

Self-awareness can be one of our greatest enemies. The
moment we become our own audience, we've turned our eyes
away from God. Sometimes we focus on our own strengths and
virtues—real or imagined. We're quite pleased with ourselves,
and we imagine how impressed everyone must be with us. But
other times (and this is just as dangerous), we focus on our
faults—real or imagined. We second-guess and pick apart all
we say and do, and torment ourselves with thoughts of failure.

Trade in your self-awareness for God-awareness, and you'll
realize that within the circle of His love there's no room for
self-importance *or* self-condemnation.

*Lord, there are times I've indulged in self-exaltation, and other times
self-condemnation. Help me to focus on You instead of me. Amen.*

Bearing Grudges

"Do not seek revenge or bear a grudge against anyone . . .
but love your neighbor as yourself."

Leviticus 19:18

In 2006, ten Amish schoolgirls were shot, five of them fatally, by a crazed man, himself the father of three children, who then committed suicide. The Amish community was rocked to its core, as was the nation. The biggest shock, however, was to come later, as the community—including the victims' parents and siblings—chose to forgive the gunman, and to surround his widow and children with compassion.[1] Some critics dismissed this act of love and forgiveness as naive and unreasonable; many, however, were in awe.

Anyone familiar with the Bible knows that God demands that we not bear grudges against those who, intentionally or unintentionally, offend us. Vengeance, He says, belongs to Him alone. In fact, in Matthew 6:15, Jesus said, "If you do not forgive others their sins, your Father will not forgive your sins." What greater love can we show our Lord than to offer to others the same grace He gives to us?

Father, help me to forgive others, even if they don't ask for my
forgiveness. Let me be a true example of Christian love. Amen.

Abounding Love

Return to the LORD your God, for he is gracious and compassionate, slow to anger and abounding in love.

Joel 2:13

Curious, the young boy sat at his mother's feet as she deftly sewed tiny stitches into the pillowcase she was embroidering. When she finished her project, she sat back and smiled. "There!" she exclaimed. "It's finished!"

Her puzzled son looked from one angle, then another, at the underside of his mother's work. "But, Mom," he protested, "it's a mess!"

His mother chuckled. "Yes, when you look at it from that side, it *is* a mess. But stand up and look at it from the other side." And the boy was amazed when he saw how beautiful the finished pillowcase really was.

While we're here on earth, our lives seem to be a complete mess, much like the underside of that pillowcase—all knots and cut ends. But God sees us from the other side—from His eternal viewpoint. And, because of His great love for us and His loving act of redemption, to Him we're beautiful.

Lord, thank You for seeing me now as the finished product I'll be in heaven. And thank You for loving me now—messy knots and all. Amen.

God's Way Versus My Way

"My thoughts and My ways are above and beyond you, just as heaven is far from your reach here on earth."

Isaiah 55:9 THE VOICE

Christians are commanded to love people and lead them to salvation. But sometimes we disagree about how this should be done. We like for people to come to Jesus in a certain way. Maybe it's a walk down an aisle or reciting a certain prayer. But God doesn't draw everyone into His love in the same way.

C. S. Lewis met the living God while riding in the sidecar of his brother's motorcycle. Their destination? The zoo. He said later, "When we set out I did not believe that Jesus is the Son of God and when we reached the zoo I did."[2] It was far from a glamorous or electrifying event. Yet he went on to create some of the most profound works on the love and magnificence of God ever written, impacting untold thousands of people.

When things happen God's way, they're saturated in His love and are absolutely perfect.

I want to lead others to You, Lord. Help me remember that my ways and Your ways are not always identical. I yield to Your ways. Amen.

Let's Make a Deal

The very fact that you have lawsuits among you means you have been completely defeated already. Why not rather be wronged?

1 Corinthians 6:7

The long-running TV show *Let's Make a Deal* is silly but entertaining. At some point in each episode, the announcer walks through the audience and asks random people if they'll make a quick deal: "I'll give you three hundred dollars for a safety pin." What a trade! Who would argue with that?

The trade from today's verse—allowing yourself to be wronged rather than bringing disgrace to the body of Christ—seems like a difficult exchange, perhaps even a bad deal. Yet the payoff of pleasing God is priceless.

When you've been wronged, if you do as Paul advised by choosing to forgive, cut your losses, and move on, you'll have the joy of fostering unity and love in the body. This verse relates not only to lawsuits, but also to disagreements between believers. Essentially, Paul was saying, "Let it go. Choose to love, retain the relationship, and honor the name of God." That's a *good* deal.

Help me, Lord, to take the high ground, extend forgiveness, cut my losses, and retain relationships even when it costs me, for the glory of Your name. Amen.

Broken

The LORD is close to the brokenhearted and saves those who are crushed in spirit.

Have you ever stood in an attic or basement that was so pitch-dark you could barely see your hand in front of your face—except for a shaft of light pouring in through a tiny crack? Did all your focus turn to that light? That's a natural reaction. And for someone who's ever been accidentally stuck in a dark attic or basement, that single beam of light quickly becomes a source of hope and promise of rescue.

Sometimes a heart can get dark inside, much like a gloomy basement or attic. When that happens, the Lord often allows that heart to be broken, to crack so that His light and life and love can shine inside. Those who've experienced deep heartbreak, sorrow, or suffering will tell you that even though the breaking process seemed endless and tortuous, their hearts were restored and renewed in the end.

Is your heart breaking? Look for the light of God's love.

Thank You, Lord, for using the broken places to introduce Your light, love, and hope into a dark situation. Amen.

Do You Love Him?

"Love the Lord your God with all your heart and with all your soul and with all your mind and with all your strength."

Mark 12:30

Do you believe in God?

Most people are pretty comfortable with this question. In fact, even those who give very little thought to God will often say they believe in Him.

Do you love God?

This is the question many people find awkward. Even many professing Christians are uncomfortable with the idea of feeling deep affection for God—though we're commanded to do so again and again.

God asks us to love Him with all our hearts and souls, the very core of who we are. We're also to love Him with our minds, to set our thoughts on Him continually. And we're to love Him with all our strength—to "throw ourselves into it," so to speak, and truly engage our whole being. In many things we should exercise moderation, but not in our love for God. He deserves our everything: our allegiance, our obedience, and all our love.

So . . . do you love God?

Lord, I want to love You more and more each day, and I want to be completely unashamed of my love for You. Amen.

Why Do You Love Him?

He leads me beside quiet waters, he refreshes my soul. He guides me along the right paths.

Psalm 23:2–3

ow that we've established that you *do* love God, here's the next question to think about: *Why?*

If someone asked you why you love your child, parent, or spouse, you might give a general answer: "She's a wonderful person." But a specific one would reveal far more about your relationship: "I love how she's so patient and gentle with children"; "I love that he's so quick to laugh at himself"; "I love him for putting integrity before monetary success."

Why, exactly, do you love God? Because He saved you from sin and death? Because He purchased your salvation and promises you heaven? Those are great answers! But what about the specifics? "I love Him for giving me the strength to get through chemotherapy"; "I love the way He surrounds me every time I walk in the woods"; "I love Him for leading me to a job I love."

Why do you love God?

Lord, I do love You so very much. I love the way You _____, the times You _____, and because You _____. Amen.

Extend Mercy

Grace, mercy and peace from God the Father and Christ Jesus our Lord.

2 Timothy 1:2

Ever since America fell in love with *The Jetsons* in the sixties, we've been fascinated by robots who'll do our bidding. Deep down, everyone wants a Rosie the Robot to fetch their briefcase, feed the dogs, and generally jump when they say, "Jump!"

Sometimes we try to make a Rosie out of someone who's wronged us. By refusing to fully forgive, we keep that person indebted to us. We're able to get him to do our bidding because he feels guilty, and we have the upper hand—and we like it just fine that way. As long as we don't let him forget what he did to us, he's at our mercy. While it can be difficult to let go of the control—to choose love and forgiveness at the expense of power—we're commanded to *fully* forgive.

If you've been withholding forgiveness, remember that Jesus fully forgave you. Do the same for the one who offended you.

Show me, Lord, if I've been refusing to let someone forget what he or she did to me. I choose love and forgiveness today. Amen.

Paradox

For if you live according to the flesh, you will die; but if by the Spirit you put to death the misdeeds of the body, you will live.

Romans 8:13

What would happen if Pinocchio said, "My nose is growing right now!"

If you eventually replace every single piece of a ship, is it still the same ship?

These are well-known paradoxes that have stumped people for ages and that aren't really solvable. A paradox is a seemingly contradictory statement. It seems both true and false at the same time.

Sometimes, God seems to be one paradox after another. Think about it: He invites us to die so we can have life. It's only by sharing in His sorrow that we can know true joy. We're truly free when we become slaves of righteousness. God requires us to carry a heavy load—"Whoever wants to be my disciple must . . . take up their cross"—but then promises that the load will be light—"My yoke is easy to bear" (Matthew 16:24 NIV; 11:30 NLT). Perhaps the best paradox of all: God's love undoes us even as it heals and mends us.

Lord, sometimes I don't understand You at all, but I do know the awesome power of Your glorious love! Amen.

Unashamed

Preach the word.

2 Timothy 4:2

*I*f you've ever been vocal about your Christian beliefs and love of God, you probably know how quickly some people will react negatively to your message. The enemy's goal is to silence you and chase you into hiding, and he uses people to do that. They may call you "judgmental" or "fanatical" when you speak about the things of God. It's embarrassing, and it hurts.

But realize there's a huge difference between being judgmental and being unashamed of your love for Jesus and the gospel. The difference between sharing the good news (which we're commanded to do) and passing sentence on others is night and day. But the devil will lie and try to make you second-guess your own motives and message.

Satan's goal isn't necessarily to strip a Christian of his beliefs, but to silence him, resulting in a barren faith. One of our greatest victories, then, is to get over our fears and "preach the word."

Lord, I'm unashamed of my love for You and Your love for me.
Teach me to resist the enemy when he tries to silence me. Amen.

Because God Said So

Joshua did as he was told, carefully obeying all the commands that the LORD had given to Moses.

Joshua 11:15 NLT

Because I said so."

No child likes to hear that phrase. She wants to know *why* she can't stay up for one more hour, eat another slice of pie, or go to the slumber party. She might pout in an attempt to change Mom's and Dad's minds, but sometimes a child simply needs to obey. Mom and Dad know more than she does. They must be trusted to make a loving and wise decision.

Once in a while, you might feel as if God is saying, "Because I said so." You feel Him prompting you to do a certain thing, but you have no idea why He's asking you to do so, and He doesn't seem to be offering any explanations. When this happens, you might be tempted to think He's being unreasonable. But God owes His children no explanations. Sometimes we simply have to trust in His perfect love and endless wisdom.

Help me to quickly obey when You speak, Lord, even if I don't completely understand. Amen.

Naysayers

*For the message of the cross is foolishness to those who are perishing,
but to us who are being saved it is the power of God.*

1 Corinthians 1:18

Person 1: My friend's treating me to my first plate of
sushi! She says it's yummy.

Person 2: Oh, don't eat that! It's horrible, and a waste of
money.

Person 1: Oh? What kind did you try?

Person 2: Well, I've never tried it.

Isn't it frustrating to hear negative comments from someone
who has no experience with the thing he or she is criticizing?
As long as what you're interested in isn't immoral or dangerous, don't let naysayers sway you. After all, how can someone
possibly know the drawbacks of sushi, kickboxing, home-
schooling, or anything else, if that person has no experience?

So it is regarding Jesus. Naysayers are a dime a dozen. Plenty
of people will tell you God is a fairy tale and Christianity is
foolishness. But chances are they've spent no time with Jesus
Himself. Do you want to know if the God of the Bible is a
loving, trustworthy God? Ask someone who truly knows and
loves Him.

*Protect me, Lord, from those who'd like to draw me away from You
when they don't even know You. Amen.*

Love Makes You Young

Let their flesh be renewed like a child's; let them be restored as in the days of their youth.

We put ourselves through great expense and even physical discomfort not only to look attractive, but also to appear younger. Our society doesn't accept the aging process well, much less honor it. Instead, we resist it with quick fixes, such as hair plugs, eyebrow lifts, and injections to erase wrinkles.

But one of the main causes of premature aging is sin. Living hard reveals itself in our eyes, countenance, and even posture. The love of God is the source of renewal; someone who's separated from Him isn't plugged in to that source, and it shows. The Word says, "The righteous. . . . will still bear fruit in old age, they will stay fresh and green" (Psalm 92:12, 14)—and the love of God "makes you strong like an eagle, restoring your youth (Psalm 103:5 THE VOICE).

If you want to put some spring back into your step and take a few years off your face, turn your eyes on Jesus.

Lord, thank You for Your love that makes me feel vibrant and renewed. As Your child, I have nothing to fear from the aging process. Amen.

Love, Hate, and Indifference

The LORD of Heaven's Armies . . . said, "Anyone who harms you harms my most precious possession."

Zechariah 2:8 NLT

The opposite of love is not hate, it's indifference," said author Elie Wiesel.[3]

Indifference is deadly. It says, "You're irrelevant. You don't matter enough to even evoke an emotion in me." Maybe this is why God said, "Because you are lukewarm—neither hot nor cold—I am about to spit you out of my mouth" (Revelation 3:16).

When we're indifferent to other people, we don't even consider their suffering. We walk right past the person who's hurting inside. To berate a family member is inexcusable, but we can do just as much damage by being indifferent: ignoring his needs; taking zero time to listen or spend time with her; or showing no interest in his life. (This is why some kids misbehave in extreme ways. They're saying, "I'd rather be shouted at than ignored.")

You're God's most precious possession; He's never, *ever* felt indifferent to You. Every moment of every day, you matter to Him.

Lord, show me if I've been indifferent to either You or those around me. Awaken my heart so that I love generously. Amen.

Love and Perfection

Above all, love each other deeply, because love covers over a multitude of sins.

1 Peter 4:8

According to the Gemological Institute of America, there is no such thing as a completely flawless diamond, though some are graded as Flawless because their imperfections are invisible without a powerful microscope.[4] The number of Flawless grade diamonds is remarkably small. They're very rare and can sell for dizzying amounts of money.

We'll pay good money for perfection. But in reality, there's no "perfect" except God, at least not here on earth. That's why perfectionism and relationships don't mesh well. By grace we're made holy and perfect, but on our own flawless is impossible. And when we demand perfection from the people we love, we set them up for failure. Maybe we'd stop asking for perfection if we remembered that by expecting it from someone else, we owe it to that person to become perfect ourselves. Focus instead on the perfect love and grace of God—and offer that to the ones we love.

Have I been expecting perfection from a family member or friend, Lord? Please change my heart and my expectations. Amen.

One

"May they all be one, as You, Father, are in Me and I am in You. May they also be one in Us."

John 17:21 HCSB

According to Credit.com, identity theft is so rampant that the IRS paid out nearly six billion dollars in fraudulent tax refunds in just one year.[5] It's no wonder that so many people take extra precautions to protect their identities. When it comes to financial issues, protecting your identity is a must.

Spiritually speaking, however, we need to learn to let go of our identities. We're so accustomed in our culture to developing and then protecting our sense of identity and autonomy that we forget God's will is for us to meld with Him. Jesus prayed that "the love you have for me may be in them and that I myself may be in them" (John 17:26). The Lord's design is that those around you can't tell where you end and He begins. There should be no clear line, no distinction between your "Sunday self," your "rest-of-the-week self," and Jesus. When people look at you, do they see Him?

Sculpt and shape me, Lord, until You and I are one. Amen.

Hanging on God's Every Word

Your word is a lamp for my feet, a light on my path.

When your love for someone is fresh and vibrant, you hang on her every word. You're far quicker to agree with her than with people who don't own a piece of your heart. You regard her words as relevant and clever. You might even call a friend and say, "Guess what she said? Isn't she *brilliant*?"

You also tend to want this person's opinion on every little subject. If you're facing a job offer or a tricky situation, you call her immediately: "What should I do?" As she explains her viewpoint, you listen attentively. Your mind doesn't wander. You not only permit that person to speak into your life, you *insist* on it.

Do you feel the same way about God? Do you love to hear God's voice so much that you search the Bible in order to hear it? Learn to go to Him as you do your beloved—"What should I do, Lord?"—and then gratefully take His advice.

Stir up such a love in my heart for Your voice and Your Word, Lord, that I'm desperate to hear from You every single day. Amen.

Fill Me Up, Lord

We know and rely on the love God has for us. God is love. Whoever lives in love lives in God, and God in them.

1 John 4:16

Thank goodness for K-Cup coffeemakers with their flashing lights that let us know they're running low on water. Back in the old days, when coffeemakers involved filter baskets and carafes, it was a common mistake to fill the filter with coffee grounds while forgetting to add water to the reservoir. Ten minutes later, the faint scorched smell and empty pot would remind you of your mistake. No matter what type of coffeemaker you prefer, it's impossible to pour yourself a hot cup of breakfast blend until you add water to the reservoir.

Neither can you pour out genuine love until you allow God to fill up your reservoir. You must first receive love from God Himself, with your arms wide open and your heart willing to accept all He has to give you. If you want to be effective in the kingdom, if you want to share His love, don't hesitate to gratefully and readily accept it!

If I'm resisting Your love in any way, Lord, please overcome my resistance and teach me to open my arms and heart to You. Amen.

Hibernation

She is not worried about the cold or snow.

Proverbs 31:21 THE VOICE

Crunchy leaves in stunning colors. Pumpkins, caramel apples, campfires, and hayrides.

Autumn is a splendid time of year. Isn't it strange, then, that the season can't happen unless a whole lot of living things die, hibernate, or lie dormant? God decided long ago that creation needed a season of death and sleep in order to be renewed again a few months later. This was His design and will, and therefore it's good and right.

God gives us spring and summer, but He also allows the seasons of winter and fall—not just in creation, but in our lives. We might feel tired, depressed, or that there's little to life except the mundane chores of daily life. If this resonates with you, hold on. Song of Songs 2:11 reminds us it'll eventually pass: "See! The winter is past; the rains are over and gone." Don't despise these seasons of hibernation; instead, use them to curl up in God's deep love.

I commit today to make the most of the season that's coming, Lord, and to remember that it's a gift from Your loving hand. Amen.

Sacrificial Love

Jacob was in love with Rachel and said, "I'll work for you seven years in return for your younger daughter Rachel."

Genesis 29:18

Most of us understand that sacrifice is necessary when it comes to love, but Jacob's level of commitment here is astonishing. *Seven years!* Think about where you were and what you were doing seven years ago. Most would agree that's a very long time. But Jacob was so smitten with Rachel that he made this generous offer, perhaps because he knew it was too good for Laban, his future father-in-law, to turn down.

Few people have ever had to give seven years of manual labor for the sake of a relationship, but sacrifice is crucial if we're to love others in the most Christlike way. Sacrificing for another person communicates commitment and devotion. Through it, we say, "I put your comfort, safety, and desires before my own." In other words, we say to that person what Jesus said to us when He died on the cross two thousand years ago.

Lord, may I be not just willing to make sacrifices, but be eager to do so for the people You've called me to love. Amen.

At Jesus' Feet

She had a sister called Mary, who sat at the Lord's feet listening to what he said.

Luke 10:39

Virtually the only time we see one person at another's feet is during a proposal. When a man gets down on one knee, he's humbly honoring the one he loves. Other than this, we don't spend much time at the feet of others. But Mary of Bethany did.

In Luke 10, Mary settled onto the floor, near Jesus' feet, so she could hear all He had to say. In John 11:32, while grieving her brother's death, she again "fell at his feet." In verse 2 we're told, "Mary was the one who anointed the Lord with fragrant oil and wiped His feet with her hair" (HCSB). Mary not only sat—and fell—at Jesus' feet, but she also washed them with her own hair. What love and devotion!

You can show your own love and devotion by sitting quietly at Jesus' feet . . . There's no better place to be.

Lord, I want to be like Mary of Bethany, who knew what was truly important. I come now to sit at Your feet. Amen.

Tuned In

"Ask me and I will tell you remarkable secrets you do not know about things to come."

Jeremiah 33:3 NLT

Some couples are so tuned in to each other that they finish each other's sentences. They can say more with the lift of an eyebrow than other couples can with a paragraph. Love makes us perceptive to the needs, feelings, and opinions of others.

In yesterday's reading, we learned that Mary lovingly poured oil on Jesus' feet. Most scholars agree this story is also told in Matthew 26, in which Jesus explained she did this "to prepare [Him] for burial" (v. 12). How amazing that Mary prophetically anointed Jesus' body just before His death! Did she truly know what was about to happen? Had Jesus told her of His destiny, or was she so in tune with Him that her actions lined up with what was about to play out in His life? Either could be true. Because deeply loving the Lord brings us in tune with His heart and will.

I want to be more in tune with You, Jesus, than I am with anyone on earth. Amen.

The Best Night's Sleep

So faith proceeds from hearing, as we listen to the message about God's Anointed.

Romans 10:17 THE VOICE

According to Smithsonian.com, we can learn while we sleep. If we listen to information while sleeping, our brains will not only reinforce existing memories and knowledge, they'll also recall that information more efficiently once we're awake.[6] In other words, if we read Psalm 91 and then listen to it that night, we'll know it more solidly and recall it more quickly the next day.

Do you love the Word? Then take advantage of the brain's abilities. There was a time when listening to the spoken Word of God meant spending a chunk of money on cassettes, but no more. Now it's free and as close as our smartphones. We can listen while we sleep—or as we drive, do dishes, shop for groceries, or sit by the pool.

Do you want to increase in love for God and others? Download your favorite book of the Bible before you lay your head on your pillow tonight.

I love Your Word, Lord! I am so grateful to live in a time when it's available 24/7. Amen.

Late Bloomer

"I will compensate you for the years that the locusts have eaten."

Joel 2:25 THE VOICE

Are you a late bloomer? Did you wait until middle age, or even longer, before giving your heart and life to Jesus Christ? Have you ever felt embarrassed because your grandchild has been saved longer than you have? If so, keep in mind that God created time, and therefore He's not constrained by it as we are. This means He can do more in six months with a disciple who's madly in love with Him than in sixty years with a lukewarm one.

God accepts late bloomers with open arms as readily as He accepts those who are saved in the tenth grade. If you're a recent convert, remember that your job isn't to try to make up for lost time; instead, your mission is the same as everyone else's: to follow and love Him daily. Do that one simple thing, and you might be surprised by where He leads you and what He accomplishes through you.

Thank You, Lord, for never giving up on me! I choose to join forces with You and make the most of every year I have with You. Amen.

The Nonnegotiables of Relationships

Do not be mismatched with unbelievers. For what partnership is there between righteousness and lawlessness?

2 Corinthians 6:14 HCSB

Parents know that while many topics are open for discussion, a few are not. If your teenage daughter wants to dye her hair, this might be negotiable. But if your eight-year-old son wants to move into the garage, you explain, "Living outside the house is not up for debate."

A parent having some nonnegotiables is a sign of love. Likewise, God's nonnegotiables are evidence of His love. Consider this: when it comes to choosing a mate, certain things are negotiable. The Lord's will for you might be to marry a chocolate-loving musician—or a rock-climbing accountant. Food preferences and careers are negotiable. But other things are not because He knows they would hurt or even destroy you: *Sex stays within the bonds of marriage. Being unequally yoked is a no-no. Treating one's partner with honor and respect is a must.*

Be thankful God loves us enough to say, *That's not up for debate.*

Lord, thank You for protecting me from myself by deeming some things nonnegotiable. Amen.

The Best Balm

Jesus didn't turn them away; He welcomed them, spoke of the kingdom of God to them, and brought health to those who needed healing.

Luke 9:11 THE VOICE

Some folks believe in the healing properties of essential oils, which are can be inhaled, massaged into the skin, or even ingested, depending on who you ask and what your ailment is. Other people rely on massage, chiropractic care, or specific dietary changes, while still others endorse more traditional methods for healing, such as prescription medicines. No doubt people will always disagree about what's most effective, but two things are sure: (1) we all need healing in body, soul, or spirit, and (2) love is the greatest healer of all.

God's love for us mends us from the inside out. Our love, in turn, offers healing to others. Love is the balm that soothes the human body, soul, and spirit; it benefits those who are physically sick, emotionally crushed, and spiritually broken. Do you ever wish you could do more for someone who's suffering? Give that person the medicine he or she needs most: patient, unconditional love.

Thank You, Lord, for reaching into my sick and broken places to bring healing. You're my Great Physician. Amen.

No Going Back

I have been crucified with Christ and I no longer live, but Christ lives in me.

Galatians 2:20

Butterflies are fascinating little creatures. They live on a liquid diet, taste their food with their feet, are able to see ultraviolet light, and usually live just a few weeks. And they all come from caterpillars.

As you probably remember from grade school, caterpillars go through a rather miraculous transformation to become butterflies. At that point of metamorphosis, the caterpillar is gone. A butterfly can't go back to being a caterpillar—*ever*. It's simply not possible. The butterfly might creep around on the ground a little, but it can never be a caterpillar again.

Likewise, once you're a born-again child of God, the old you is gone. Even on the days when you feel like a worm, you're redeemed, priceless, and victorious. Because Jesus loves you and gave His life for you, you're transformed by God's own Spirit. There's genuine, eternal life inside you because Jesus lives *in* you and loves *through* you.

I trust Your Word, Lord, that assures me that even on my worst days, I'm still holy in Your sight and perfectly loved by Your heart. Amen.

NOVEMBER

*"Anyone who loves me will obey my teaching.
My Father will love them, and we will come
to them and make our home with them."*

John 14:23

Do You Love Them?

When you shepherd the flock God has given you, watch over them not because you have to but because you want to.

1 Peter 5:2 THE VOICE

popular pastor explained his secret to effective teaching and preaching: before he delivers a message, he asks himself, *Do I love these people?* He realizes that, (1) even the best pastor or teacher can slip into a habit of delivering sermons out of obligation instead of love; and (2) if he doesn't love the people to whom he's offering a message, it's just words with no heart and no power. The words will fall flat, no matter how eloquent the teacher. This is why people are more impacted by a word of advice that comes from someone who genuinely loves them than the same piece of advice from someone who's knowledgeable but not emotionally invested in them or their situation.[1]

Only love will allow us to serve God's people well. Only love will bring life to our words so they have meaning. And only love has the power to penetrate hearts and produce change.

Increase my love for those I lead, Lord, so that I always speak from a heart of love. Amen.

The Power of Love

Do not despise these small beginnings, for the LORD rejoices to see the work begin.

With their doe-like faces, brawny shoulders, and powerful legs, kangaroos are both endearing and intimidating. An adult red male kangaroo can jump up to thirty-five miles per hour, and he can crush the bones of (or even kill) a rival kangaroo with a kick of his hind legs. Yet this same kangaroo is only about the size of a black olive at birth! If you saw a newborn kangaroo, you'd never suspect it could end up as a three-hundred-pound powerhouse.

Sometimes the smallest, weakest, most helpless things grow into powerhouses. While there are "baby Christians" who will spend sixty years as nominal believers, serving God as little as possible, there are others who latch on to God's promises, believing by faith that they're not only redeemed and saved but secure and utterly loved—and they grow into world-changing powerhouses. That's the power of a loving God in a faith-filled Christian. Will you let God make a powerhouse out of you?

I give You my heart, Lord. Help me hold fast to You so that I can be a champion of the faith. Amen.

Pass It Around

Slander no one . . . be peaceable and considerate, and always . . . be gentle toward everyone.

Titus 3:2

In the movie *When Calls the Heart*, the schoolteacher tries to teach her scrappy students to be kind to one another. Their assignment is to do a kindness to someone that week and then report about it to the class. The assignment has an amazing effect; the children learn that a single act of kindness can change a relationship.

In today's verse, Paul, in his letter to Titus, told Titus (and all of us) that kindness should be a constant practice in our lives, not just for a week, but "always." Imagine what would happen in our world if we all put this into practice! "Love your enemies," said Jesus (Matthew 5:44). "If your enemy is hungry, feed him; if he is thirsty, give him something to drink" (Romans 12:20). Kindness should be directed not just toward our friends and loved ones, but toward everyone, including our enemies. Pass it around!

Father, help me show loving-kindness to all who cross my path. Teach me to love as You love! Amen.

Consistency

But you remain the same, and your years will never end.

Hebrews 1:12

Every time there's a change of administration in America, for a few months there's also considerable confusion and turmoil. As the new administration chooses its cabinet and the heads of governmental departments, Congress and the other powers that be jostle for influence and try to ascertain the new leaders' positions on policies. Meanwhile, the country holds its breath in either expectation or dread. *Where is the nation going now?* we all wonder.

With God, however, there's no confusion, no uncertainty, no indecision, and no changes. He's the same today as He was yesterday and will be tomorrow. There will be no revisions to His laws or alterations in His truths. Without exception, we can know with complete certainty what's right and what's wrong and what He expects of us. Because He loves us so much, God stays the same—faithful and true; merciful and just; all-knowing, all-powerful, and all-loving. Forever.

Lord, thank You for being a consistent God; thank You for the promise that Your truths and laws will never change. Amen.

Loving What God Loves

You made both summer and winter.

When you love someone, you learn to love what he loves, and you care about what brings her joy. Maybe you like to stay close to home on the weekends and catch up on chores, but your closest friend loves canoeing. So you venture onto the water for his sake. No, you're not crazy about canoeing, but you love making your friend happy.

It's the same way with God. When we love Him, we do our best to care about what He cares about. This applies to big issues, such as justice for the poor, but it's just as true when it comes to smaller, day-to-day things. For example, you might dread the coming of winter, but this year you determine to remember that God created and put His stamp of approval on every season, including winter. So you bundle up and go outside. You seek Him . . . and discover the joy of stomping through drifts and making snow angels.

Jesus, I want to bring You joy every day, so help me love the things You love. Amen.

The Lord's Fight

The LORD will fight for you; you need only to be still.

Exodus 14:14

ave you ever been accused of something you didn't do? Your first reaction was probably to exclaim, rather loudly, "I didn't do it!" You want to fight to preserve your reputation. But sometimes God asks you to be still.

As Moses led the Hebrew people out of their slavery in Egypt, Pharaoh gathered his army and gave chase. When he cornered the Hebrews between the Red Sea and the desert, the people complained that they were now in an even worse situation than they'd been as slaves. "Do not be afraid," Moses told them. "Stand firm and you will see the deliverance of the LORD" (Exodus 14:13). He didn't tell them to take up arms and fight back. He told them to stand firm and let *God* fight for them! And the Lord did—taking them safely through the sea and completely destroying Pharaoh and his army.

When you're facing a battle, don't be afraid. Stand firm, and let the God who loves you fight for you.

You're faithful and true, Lord, and I place my trust in You. Help me to be still as You fight for me. Amen.

Because He Loves

When the Israelites saw the mighty hand of the LORD displayed against the Egyptians, the people feared the LORD and put their trust in him.

Exodus 14:31

If you pray for a miracle, what's your reaction if the miracle does *not* occur? Do you get angry at God, give up on praying, or wonder what you said or did wrong?

A heartbroken mother prayed for reconciliation with her estranged daughter for thirty-nine years. She never got angry at God or blamed Him. And she never gave up, knowing God's response to her prayers would be according to *His* perfect will. In the thirty-ninth year, God worked out a joyous reconciliation.

God doesn't always answer our prayers the way we think He should, when we want Him to, or in the way we ask. Sometimes He has better plans, or He waits to see if we'll trust Him and continue asking Him for help, or He knows the timing isn't right. Because God loves us, He does what's best for us. And He does what's best for us because He loves us.

I know, Lord, that even though You don't always answer my prayers when or how I want, You are giving me the very best answer. Amen.

You're Not That Fast

Where shall I flee from your presence? If I ascend to heaven, you are there!

Psalm 139:7–8 ESV

*I*n 2014 at the Berlin Marathon, Dennis Kimetto of Kenya broke the world record by running 26.2 miles in 2:02:57, shaving a full 26 seconds off the prior world record.[2] The average time for a male marathoner is more than twice Kimetto's time!

But no one, no matter how fast, can outrun God's love. We can resist and push people away until they're fed up, but we cannot wear God out, and we can't run beyond the scope of His offered grace. He will pursue us until the end. Poet Francis Thompson called God the "Hound of Heaven," and J. F. X. O'Conor explained the name this way: "As the hound follows the hare, never ceasing in its running, ever drawing nearer . . . so does God follow the fleeing soul by His Divine grace."[3]

The best thing we can do is stop, surrender, and receive God and all that He has for us. We'll never regret a choice like that.

Lord, forgive me for the times I've run away from You. I surrender. I am Yours. Amen.

The Gift of Alone Time

The next morning, Jesus sneaks away. He finds a place away from the crowds.

Luke 4:42 THE VOICE

One of the greatest gifts we can give ourselves is permission to stop and spend some alone time with God. This is especially true if you've been pushing yourself extra hard, working long hours, or dealing with a difficult person or situation. To need this time isn't a character flaw; it's a perfectly normal requirement for any human being. And the best way for any overextended, weary person to refuel is through time alone to simply *be*, with no distractions or demands.

Would you be willing to reserve a campsite or a room at a bed-and-breakfast and then spend a long weekend fishing or window shopping, with only the Lord to keep you company? Does just the idea make you feel guilty? Remember the world will keep spinning without you. Stop and allow God to love you by refreshing and renewing you. Don't miss out by wrongly convincing yourself that you're the one person who doesn't need alone time with Him.

Lord, help me not to feel guilty about spending time alone with You. In fact, help me to hunger for it and make room for it in my schedule. Amen.

To the Moon and Back

He chose us in him before the creation of the world. . . . In love he predestined us for adoption to sonship.

Ephesians 1:4–5

Have you ever been in the company of two kids but offered a compliment to just one of them? This can be a tricky situation. The moment you say, "That was a wonderful somersault," to Child Number 1, Child Number 2 feels snubbed. "What about me?" she wails. "I can do a somersault too!"

Kids don't understand that when an adult offers love and approval to one child, it doesn't diminish the love that parent feels for another child. Unfortunately, some Christians never quite seem to outgrow this mind-set. We see God's blessing on someone's life, and instead of rejoicing, we get snippy and spiteful. But God doesn't need to ration His love. He's infinite, and so are His attributes—including love. If there were a billion times a billion humans alive at this moment, God would love each one of us to the moon and back.

Your never-ending capacity to love is astonishing, Lord. Forgive me for any time I've been jealous of the love and blessings You pour out on others. Amen.

Soldiers

Then the officers shall add, "Is anyone afraid or fainthearted? Let him go home so that his fellow soldiers will not become disheartened too."

Deuteronomy 20:8

*C*ombat. What a fearful word! Those of us who have never been in the midst of war can't begin to imagine the horrors that our military men and women face as they serve in combat. But we can serve them by honoring them with our prayers.

When God tells us we're to love others as we love ourselves, He doesn't exclude our military personnel. In fact, there are numerous times in the Bible when He performed extraordinary, supernatural feats to help Israel's armies win battles.

On Veterans' Day we acknowledge and honor the brave people who have served in the U.S. Army, Navy, Marines, Air Force, Coast Guard, and National Guard. In this way, and by our prayers, we demonstrate our love, respect, and appreciation for the sacrifices they make for each of us. God bless all those who serve!

Father God, put Your hedge of protection around each of our servicemen and -women. And bless those who stay home while their loved ones serve. Amen.

Love and Purity

I made a covenant with my eyes not to look lustfully at a young woman.

Job 31:1

What's your favorite indulgence? French fries? Pizza with real mozzarella? Hot fudge sundaes? If you've ever given up that favorite food for a diet or other reasons, you know you didn't magically start hating the taste of it when you decided to quit eating it! Choosing to abstain for the greater good didn't change your desires, but by standing strong you were able to hold your appetite in check.

So it is regarding purity. The desire to be sexually pure begins with a love for God and His ways. God's love and strength enable the unmarried Christian to abstain for the greater good. As Eric Liddell wrote, "Purity . . . [means] having the instincts as servants and not the master of the spirit."[4] Rather than allowing our instincts and desires to boss us around, we force them to take a back seat to our allegiance to God—so that true love reigns.

You know, Lord, about my struggles and temptations. May love and purity reign in my life. Amen.

The Fog of War

"Not by might nor by power, but by my Spirit," says the LORD Almighty.

Zechariah 4:6

*F*og of war is a military term for the utter confusion that happens when warfare is very intense, when a soldier is so disoriented that he hardly knows where he is. During the fog of war, commanders can discover they're clueless as to where the enemy is, where their allies are, and who's winning the battle. It's a terrifying and bewildering experience.

Ordinary life can also be so full of battles that we find ourselves in a fog. But there's hope: we have an Ally and Friend—a Commander—who never loses track of us, even when we feel as if we've lost track of Him. In the midst of smoke and whizzing bullets, when everything feels upside down, He's by your side, saying, *I know exactly what's happening. I know right where you are because you're in My heart. I know your future. I've got everything under control. Just breathe.*

In those moments when I want to ask, "Where did You go, Lord?" I'll trust that You have every single thing under control. Amen.

Would You Rather?

I would rather be a doorkeeper in the house of my God than dwell in the tents of the wicked.

Psalm 84:10

In the fourteenth century, doorkeepers served as prison guards, and, though we don't see them as much today, they do still serve the House of Commons in England. Today their tasks range from delivering important messages to acting as security guards. And, ever since smoking was banned from the House of Commons in the 1690s, doorkeepers have also maintained a box of snuff for the convenience of members and officials.

But David wasn't concerned with snuff and security when he said he'd rather be a doorkeeper in God's house than live comfortably with evil companions. Essentially, he was saying that to have even the smallest place in God's kingdom was inexpressibly better than being honored by those who didn't know God or His love. But the truth is that we're not simple doorkeepers in God's sight; we're His beloved children. And He has a place in His kingdom prepared just for us (John 14:2).

Just like David, I'd rather be a doorkeeper in Your house, Lord, than to live without You for even a moment. Amen.

Perception Versus Reality

It is to one's honor to avoid strife, but every fool is quick to quarrel.

Proverbs 20:3

It's a terrible feeling: you walk into the breakroom, and a coworker stifles a giggle as everyone else abruptly stops talking. All day, you feel as if people are avoiding you.

Why's everyone's acting like they've got a secret? you wonder. *Maybe I'm about to get fired! What if I did something stupid without realizing it?*

Perception is a powerful thing. But because perception is all about interpretation, it's sometimes even *more* powerful than fact. Haven't we all tortured ourselves, worrying about something we perceived in the wrong way? In that breakroom scenario, the big secret might be a surprise birthday party—for you.

Often, perception and reality are worlds apart. Remember this the next time you face a conflict with someone. If he or she is using phrases such as, "That's not what I meant" or, "You don't get what I'm saying," consider that your perception might be a little skewed. Choose to love by taking one more look at the situation.

Lord, do I often interpret what others do or say in the wrong way?
If so, please tweak my perception and keep me from causing strife.
Amen.

This Is Worship

[Abraham] said to his servants, "Stay here with the donkey while I and the boy go over there. We will worship and then we will come back to you."

Genesis 22:5

Let him go, Daughter.

The young woman knew she was hearing the Lord's gentle voice. She broke down in tears, already grieving the end of a relationship with a man she had once hoped to marry. Crumpling to her knees, she took a deep breath and answered, "Yes, Lord."

This is worship.

The first time the word *worship* is used in the Bible is just after God has told Abraham to sacrifice his beloved son, and just before Abraham heads up the mountain where the sacrifice is to take place. Who knows what might have been going through Abraham's mind? Some assume he was confident that God would come through at the last minute, and that's definitely a possibility. But isn't it also possible Abraham was battling fear and grief? Either way, this scene is about sacrifice and teaches us about the heart of true worship: submission to God. He speaks, and we obey—no matter the cost.

This is worship.

Lord, is there someone or something I need to let go of? Give me the strength to worship You with my obedience. Amen.

Playing with Fire

*Submit yourselves to the one true God and fight against the devil
and his schemes. If you do, he will run away in failure.*

James 4:7 THE VOICE

In 2013, a Georgia fire department was doing a controlled burn when it went amiss and swept through a family's backyard, engulfing several sheds containing an antique porcelain doll collection. In 2014, in California, embers from a quietly burning fire set by a landowner were swept up by the wind, destroying hundreds of acres. A controlled burn is often beneficial, but turn your back for thirty seconds, and you might be calling the fire department.

Sometimes, Christians face crises they didn't anticipate because there are many ways to play with fire: Spending time with a friend who's so much "fun" she makes it easy to sin. Accidentally landing on a pornographic website—and then staying there. Indulging in a "harmless" flirtation with a married coworker.

At the first sign of temptation, err on the side of caution. Never turn your back when it comes to honoring the Lord and maintaining your relationship with Him.

*May I never play with fire when it comes to my relationship with
You, Lord. Protect me from temptation. Amen.*

Love Letters

My heart is stirred by a noble theme . . . My tongue is the pen of a skillful writer.

r. Billy Graham was once asked if reading the Bible was really that important. He responded, "The Bible is God's 'love letter' to us, telling us not only that He loves us, but showing us what He has done to demonstrate His love."[5] Most would agree with Dr. Graham's assessment about the Word of God. But have you ever thought about writing a love letter to the Lord in return?

You probably have various ways of expressing your love for God. Maybe you like to sing, or you've committed to obey Him quickly to show Him that you're devoted to Him. But if you enjoy writing—even if you're no C. S. Lewis—consider journaling your thoughts and prayers. Be honest and transparent, writing exactly what's on your heart. You might never share your writings with another human being, but that's part of the beauty of it! Love letters aren't to be shared with anyone but your beloved.

Thank You for the amazing love letter of the Bible, Lord. If I were to write a love letter to You, this is the first thing I would say: _____. Amen.

Infinite Grace

We all believe that we will be liberated through the grace of the Lord Jesus.

Acts 15:11 THE VOICE

In the charming and much-loved television program *The Andy Griffith Show*, Sheriff Andy and his bumbling deputy, Barney Fife, were the entire police force of the town of Mayberry. The long-suffering sheriff spent much of his time encouraging and gently correcting Barney. In fact, he could not even allow Barney to carry a loaded pistol, for fear his deputy would shoot an innocent bystander—or the tires of the patrol car. So Barney toted an unloaded gun, with one bullet in his shirt pocket.

Sheriff Andy was the epitome of grace. With love, patience, and good humor, he graciously nudged Barney in the right direction.

Our God is a God of infinite grace. As we bumble our way along through life, He's always there, lovingly, patiently, and obviously with good humor coaxing us in the right direction. What incredible love He must have for us to lavish us with His grace!

Father God, thank You for giving me so much grace. Teach me to give that same kind of grace to everyone around me. Amen.

All Year Long

Whoever is kind to the poor lends to the LORD, and he will reward them for what they have done.

Proverbs 19:17

The holidays are upon us! Soon, churches all over the country will be hosting Thanksgiving dinner for the homeless. In another month, people will "adopt" low-income children and bless them with toys. People will bring home and dote on elderly family members they don't often see.

The heart of God is pleased when someone reaches out to the poor, lonely, sick, or hungry during this season. However, we should never forget that hunger, poverty, illness, and loneliness are just as devastating in February and March and July as they are on Thanksgiving and Christmas Day.

Love is willing to invest on a consistent basis. It doesn't offer a token act of kindness and then move on. It refuses to forget about the suffering of others. This doesn't mean you must launch into full-time missions or give half your paycheck to the poor. But it does mean finding ways to love those in need, all year long.

Don't allow me forget the sick or the lonely or the poor once this holiday season is over, Lord. May I love them as You do—always. Amen.

Best Friend Forever

The soul of Jonathan was knit to the soul of David, and Jonathan loved him as his own soul.

1 Samuel 18:1 ESV

A close friendship is something to be desired and cherished. Having a "BFF," a "best friend forever," is truly a blessing. In Old Testament times, however, friendships that were deep and lasting sometimes went far beyond most friendships today, as the people involved would enter into a covenant, binding them together for life. Jonathan and David entered into such a covenant. In effect, they swore to each other, "What's mine is yours—my property, my money, my debts, my responsibilities. If you're in danger, I'll come to your aid. If something happens to you, I'll care for your family forever."

After Jonathan died, David became king, but he still kept his covenant promise and cared for Jonathan's disabled son, Mephibosheth. He treated Mephibosheth as one of his own sons, even having him eat at his own table. Such was the depth of the love between David and Jonathan. Would you do as much for your best friend?

Father God, create in me a heart of love, and teach me to be committed to my friends—in good times and in times of need. Amen.

Love Gives Freely

Now teach these truths to other trustworthy people who will be able to pass them on to others.

2 Timothy 2:2 NLT

We can get great joy out of passing on our skills and knowledge. Maybe you've shared lots of cooking tips with your sister. Or perhaps you taught your grandparents the basics of computers so they could navigate Facebook and message their old classmates.

But is it a difficult pill to swallow if your student eventually knows more than you do? How would you feel if your former Sunday school student, whom you introduced to the Lord and then discipled, ended up with more speaking engagements than you could ever hope for?

When we realize we've freely received from God more than we can ever repay, we'll be happy to give freely to others. We'll refuse to hoard knowledge, even if that means our students will accomplish more than we have, or be even more effective than we are. In fact, we'll rejoice when they pass us up, knowing we've done our job well.

Lord, teach me to love others by freely passing on the things You've taught me and by sharing the gifts and skills You've blessed me with. Amen.

A Love That Sacrifices

Where you go I will go, and where you stay I will stay. Your people will be my people and your God my God.

Relationships today are often rocky at best. Best friends betray each other; marriages end in divorce; parents and children are at odds. Perhaps that's because so many relationships are based on self-gratification rather than love: *What can I get out of this?* And far too often those relationships end because one person or the other refuses to sacrifice his or her selfish desires for the other's benefit.

The story of Ruth is one example of a love that sacrifices. Naomi, Ruth's mother-in-law, had lost her husband and both of her sons, leaving her alone in a foreign land with her two daughters-in-law. So Naomi decided to move from Moab back to her home in Bethlehem. As they were on their way, Naomi urged the two young widows to turn around and go back to their own families. Ruth, however, chose to stay with Naomi. She sacrificed home, family, and everything she knew to stay with Naomi—a wonderful example of a love that sacrifices.

Lord, teach me to love as Ruth loved and to be willing to sacrifice my own desires out of love for another. Amen.

The "Opener"

If you seek him, he will be found by you.

1 Chronicles 28:9

Have you ever used a letter opener? It's a simple, inexpensive little gadget that prevents tearing an envelope to shreds while trying to open it. But did you know you also have another kind of "letter opener" who's always with you, requires no PhD to use, and helps you free of charge? It's the Holy Spirit. When you become a child of God, the Holy Spirit actually resides within you. He's always available, requires no special knowledge to contact, and doesn't cost you a thing.

The Holy Spirit will help you open up the letter of God's Word and better understand it. If you're struggling with a passage, ask Him for revelation. As today's verse says, if you seek the Lord, you *will* find Him. Guaranteed.

God wants you—and every person on earth—to seek Him, get to know Him, have a personal relationship with Him, and understand His Word—and His Spirit is the opener you need.

Thank You, Lord, for sending the Holy Spirit to be with me. I believe that when I seek You, I will find You. Amen.

Supernatural Protection

Daniel was taken out of the [lions'] den, uninjured, for he trusted in his God.

Daniel 6:23 HCSB

Daniel, a young Hebrew man, was a devout believer in the God of Israel. Taken as a slave to Babylon, he was chosen to be a special servant to the Babylonian king. But some were jealous of Daniel and conspired against him. They succeeded in tricking the king, forcing him to throw Daniel into a lions' den (a common punishment in their time). But Daniel reassured the distraught king that his God would take care of him. The next morning, the king hurried to the den and called out, asking Daniel if his God had, indeed, taken care of him. Daniel came out of the den uninjured, "for he trusted in his God."

Our Lord is a God of supernatural power and protection. What seems impossible to us is easy to Him. When we trust God, He'll bring His power to work in our lives—because He loves us.

Dear Lord, the story of Daniel reminds me that nothing is impossible for You. I am amazed by Your great love and power. Amen.

How Do I Love Thee?

Praise him with the sounding of the trumpet, praise him with the harp and lyre.

Psalm 150:3

Elizabeth Barrett Browning's *Sonnets from the Portuguese* consists of forty-four love sonnets. "How Do I Love Thee?" is perhaps her best known. People have been creating poems for thousands of years, and we can only guess how many books have been written about romantic love—yet no one has quite captured what it feels like. As wonderful as words are, they don't quite cut it. That's why people throughout the ages have tried to express love in other ways—for example, through heroic acts or extravagant gifts.

Have you ever found it difficult to accurately describe God's love for you—or yours for Him? If so, feel free to express your love for Him in other ways, perhaps with raised hands or dropped to your knees. When words are insufficient, speak through a melody; create a painting or drawing; or, since some things are so wonderful they require silence, simply sit in His company without saying a word.

My words are insufficient, Lord, to tell You how I feel about You. See my heart, and help me express what's inside. Amen.

Air Cover

Take up the shield of faith, with which you can extinguish all the flaming arrows of the evil one. . . . Always keep on praying for all the Lord's people.

Ephesians 6:16, 18

In military terms, *air cover* is the "protective use of military aircraft during ground operations."[6] Air cover supports ground troops and gives them as much protection from the enemy as possible.

Christians need air cover too. One of the most loving things you can do for a fellow believer is to provide air cover through prayer—especially if that person is in a position of leadership, as God's leaders are prime targets for the enemy, Satan. You can greatly assist the ground troops (those who labor in the kingdom daily) by covering their backs and offering support through prayer. You can also assist the captives (those who are still lost and without God) by praying they find the kingdom.

If you'd like to cover your leaders in prayer but aren't sure what they need, just ask. Love them well by sacrificing a bit of time each day for intercession. They'll sense your prayers and appreciate the holy air cover.

Each day, Lord, please bring someone to mind for whom You'd like me to pray. Amen.

Your God, My God

I am convinced that nothing can ever separate us from God's love.

Romans 8:38 NLT

Your friend can never make up her mind about people. One week she adores her spouse ("He's such a blessing from God!") and the next, she's comparing him to the devil ("Selfish man! I'd hate to be him on Judgment Day!"). Her feelings for friends, coworkers, and siblings also vacillate. But the strangest thing is that, in her estimation, these people are on God's good side only when they're on *her* good side!

Author Anne Lamott's friend Tom once told her, "You can safely assume you've created God in your own image when it turns out that He hates all the same people you do."[7] Sometimes we assume that if we don't like someone, then neither does God.

Never forget that the One who extends mercy and a million chances to us does the same for those with whom we don't see eye to eye. Loving others means acknowledging that our compassionate God is *their* compassionate God as well.

Lord, thank You for being so good, not just to me, but to everyone, including _____. Amen.

What'll It Be?

"Listen, listen to me, and eat what is good, and you will delight in the richest of fare."

Isaiah 55:2

You've finally saved up enough money to take your dearest friend to the best restaurant in town. The food is superb, and the menu includes several of your friend's favorites: lobster ravioli, fire-roasted pizza, and chicken marsala. You can't wait to treat him to whatever he wants. As you settle into the booth, you ask, "So, what'll it be?"

"Oh, I'm fine," he answers. "I'm not hungry. You go ahead and eat, though."

It's just as absurd to go to a church service and not desire time with God as it is to go to the finest restaurant and refuse to order. Do you get so caught up in your Sunday morning responsibilities that you forget to expect an encounter with God? Or are you so busy praying for everyone around you that you've forgotten you need Him too? God loves you and delights in blessing you. Ask Him for what you need—He's waiting to answer.

Forgive me, Lord, for failing to anticipate an encounter with You every time I walk through the doors of Your church. Amen.

Can You Hear Him?

"You are precious in my eyes, and honored, and I love you."

Isaiah 43:4 ESV

D o you hear the Lord when He speaks to your heart? If so, what does He say most often?

Don't be afraid.

I'm right here.

Be careful.

I wish you wouldn't do that.

Show that person some compassion.

How about *I love you*? Do you hear Him say that? Because He definitely says it.

When we're tuned in to God's expressions of love, we find that insecurity disappears. When we truly believe that our Creator is crazy about us, we'll rest in that great love and stop wallowing in self-doubt and anxiety. We'll also stop looking to our loved ones to make us feel whole, accepted, and validated. Even the people we're closest to can't give us what we ultimately need: the flawless, all-encompassing love that only God can supply.

Can you hear the Lord? Listen, He's saying it again: *I love you*.

I'm listening, Lord. Please open my ears to hear You whispering, "I love you." Amen.

DECEMBER

....

But I trust in your unfailing love; my
heart rejoices in your salvation.

Psalm 13:5

Performing the Work with Love

Whatever your hand finds to do, do it with all your might.

Ecclesiastes 9:10

Brother Lawrence, who learned to dwell in God's presence even as he washed dishes for hours at a time, wrote, "We ought not to be weary of doing little things for the love of God, who regards not the greatness of the work, but the love with which it is performed."[1]

A good teacher can turn out students who excel in their studies, but the best teacher asks himself, *How can I show these kids the love of Christ even as I talk about polygons?* A short-order cook who flies through her tickets is well worth her paycheck, but the best cook prays for her customers even as she cracks their eggs.

There are lots of fine reasons that people excel at their jobs: a good work ethic, a desire to please, the ambition to move up. But none compare with the desire to love the people you serve.

Show me, Lord, how to not just do my work, but to do it so that Your love shines through to those I serve. Amen.

One-on-One

The LORD would speak to Moses face to face, as one speaks to a friend.

Exodus 33:11

The grandmother treasured all her grandkids. When they were all together, she enjoyed the happy chaos. But her favorite custom was to spend one-on-one time with each of them. That way, she could focus her time and affection on a particular child's preferences and personality. For example, her six-year-old grandson knew that "Grandma weekend" meant ham and Fritos sandwiches, Play-Doh, and dinosaur movies—little indulgences done just for him.

To love someone well—whether a grandchild, friend, spouse, or parent—one-on-one time is crucial. Have you ever considered that God wants to share some moments with only *you*? That He wants to spend some one-on-one time relating to you in a way that fits your unique personality?

Don't neglect one-on-one time with God. Corporate worship and prayer are wonderful and necessary, but make time each day to sit down with God or take a walk alone with Him . . . just as you would anyone else you dearly love.

I love the fact that You want to spend time with just me. Help me to make that a priority every day. Amen.

Right Perception

For the wise can see where they are going, but fools walk in the dark.
Ecclesiastes 2:14 NLT

There's an entertaining TV show on the Discovery Channel called *Canada's Worst Driver* in which a handful of the worst drivers in the country come together and then go through intensive training in driving skills. Invariably, these accident-prone individuals are either overconfident or underconfident. Their perceptions of their driving skills are inaccurate, and the results are disastrous. It seems the best drivers are those who are attuned to their own strengths *and* weaknesses.

Similarly, to get through life without a spiritual disaster, Christians need to have an accurate perception of themselves—one that's neither overconfident nor insecure. If we eagerly receive God's perfect love, we won't get caught up in pride *or* self-condemnation. Instead, we'll rest in the peace of knowing we're perfectly loved. We won't crash due to overconfidence because we'll be aware of how easily and often we still sin—but we also won't be stalled out by fear because we'll know we're safe in the grip of God's loving grace.

Please give me a right perception of how perfectly loved and how weak I am without Your strength, Lord. Amen.

Go to the River

There is a river whose streams make glad the city of God, the holy place where the Most High dwells.

Psalm 46:4

You've probably heard the metaphor that you can memorize a driver's handbook cover to cover, ride along with someone as he drives, watch people drive all day long on TV—but until you've gotten behind the wheel and steered a car down the road on your own, you have *not* driven.

We can also apply this concept to the spiritual life. We can read a hundred books about having a relationship with God, we can watch movies in which people love God enough to die for Him, and we can hear countless sermons about the Christian life. But ultimately, no one can interact with the living God *for* us. As one preacher said, "There are things you must go to the river and get from God Himself."[2] No one will go for you, because the God who loves you wants you to know Him, not just know *about* Him.

Lord, don't let me settle for simply knowing about You. Help me to dive into the river of You and truly get to know You. Amen.

Lead Them to Jesus

"Good teacher," he asked, "what must I do to inherit eternal life?"

Mark 10:17

Think of all the things we adults do for the kids in our lives. Parents and caregivers do virtually everything for them when they're babies! When they're four, we no longer have to change diapers, but we still feed, clothe, and nurture them constantly. Preschool teachers share the gift of learning with them. Even in their teens, when they can do many things for themselves, coaches lead them in practice, tutors help with homework, and grandparents give lots of advice. The list is endless.

But there's one thing we'll never be able to do for them no matter how much we love them: we'll never be able to receive God's love and offer of salvation in their stead. Only they can do that. But *we* must lead them to Jesus. We'll make some mistakes—everyone does—but don't make the mistake of failing to direct children to God. Love these kids by introducing them to—and then teaching them about—their Savior.

Guide me, Lord, as I guide the children in my life to You and then teach them about You daily. Amen.

Love Out Loud

A well-spoken word at just the right moment is like golden apples in settings of silver.

Proverbs 25:11 THE VOICE

What would I do without my sister? I love her so much! He's the most big-hearted person I've ever met.

We all have a million thoughts each day that we don't express. For the most part, that's fine—we can't (and shouldn't) articulate every thought that skips through our brain. But some thoughts do need to be said out loud.

If you were to ask the typical man, "Have you ever thought, *My wife is the most patient woman in the world*, or, *She's so great with the kids?*" many would say yes—while admitting that voicing those thoughts had never occurred to them. Ask the typical adult if there's a coworker whose patience, humor, or work ethic makes the office a better place and most would say yes, yet many have never articulated their feelings.

The next time your heart swells with affection or appreciation for someone, say it—love out loud.

Please bring to my remembrance, Lord, the value of telling the people around me all the little ways I love them. Amen.

Love in Action

Dear children, let us not love with words or speech but with actions and in truth.

1 John 3:18

The Smiths just lost everything in a fire," the woman told her ten-year-old daughter. "Let's get busy." Together, mother and daughter cleaned out closets and sold dozens of items on eBay. They cashed in the penny jar and launched a crowdfunding campaign. A few days later, they took $600 and a batch of homemade cookies to their neighbors.

A year later, the daughter still remembered the experience as though it had happened yesterday.

The best way to teach a child to be a loving adult is through example—and not just allowing them to watch what we do, but actually carrying out simple acts of kindness themselves. A kindergartener can learn to share with a new baby sister. A tween can enjoy passing out bingo cards at the senior center. A teenager with a landscaping business can feel the satisfaction of mowing one yard each week for free just because.

Don't just tell or show children how to love; let them learn by doing.

Kind Father, please give me creative ideas for how to teach the children in my life how to love others. Amen.

Roadblocks

"Return to me," declares the LORD Almighty, "and I will return to you."

Zechariah 1:3

𝓘n August 2010, traffic in Beijing, China, backed up for an appalling sixty-two miles. Some people were stuck in their cars for days. Clever entrepreneurs even took advantage of the situation, selling water and noodles for ridiculous prices. The whole mess was caused by a construction roadblock.[3]

Relationship roadblocks can cause messes too. They can divide us from friends and family. And they can seriously obstruct our intimacy with God. We're cruising along in God's love, but then one day we can't remember the last time we were excited about our Christian walk. Somewhere along the way we got stuck, and we haven't moved forward in six months.

A spiritual roadblock might involve an overloaded schedule, a relationship that doesn't honor God, a tainted conscience, or an unhealthy mind-set, such as self-pity. Is there a barricade in your path to greater intimacy with God? Do whatever it takes to get unstuck and be on your way.

Lord, I don't want anything getting in the way of my love and devotion to You. Help me recognize roadblocks and deal with them instantly. Amen.

Silent Prayers

Let my voice reach You! Please listen to my prayers!

*D**ear God, I'm so lonely.*
    Lord, I don't mean to be harsh. I love my family so much.
    Please, God, help me stop drinking. I'm such a failure!
    So often, Lord, I feel like this world would be a better place without me.

What if we could hear the silent prayers that God hears? Would we have more insight and compassion when it comes to those difficult-to-love people in our lives?

Sometimes, the people who are the most challenging experience deep pain on a daily basis. Yes, sometimes they're simply reaping what they've sown. Even so, if we could hear the prayers that they whisper, we'd probably find it easier to be patient and kind. We might even be able to relate to what they're dealing with. The next time you're struggling to show Christlike love to someone infuriating, ask the Lord for insight as to what's truly inside his or her heart.

Lord, you hear the prayers that _____ prays at night. Please show me how to best love him or her. Amen.

Different Versus Flawed

Those who don't eat certain foods must not condemn those who do,
for God has accepted them.

Romans 14:3 NLT

Which is better: risk-taker or safety conscious? Methodical or whimsical? Leader or follower? Studious or artistic? Open-handed or thrifty?

The answer is neither—although most people do associate certain traits with good and others with bad. Perhaps that's because we tend to view things (and people) who are different than we are as flawed. But love refuses to do this. Love understands that *different* isn't synonymous with *defective*.

Think about it: we even view food this way! If we're unfamiliar with kumquats (or anchovies or oysters), we immediately reject them. "Eww!" we say. "Kumquats are disgusting!" There's not much harm in thinking of kumquats as flawed, but it's another thing when it comes to our neighbors. If you're a stay-at-home mom and she's a career woman, or if you're reserved and he's demonstrative, honor the fact that he or she is different—and then think of what a boring world this would be if everyone were the same!

Lord, please show me if I've misjudged other people simply because
they're different from me. Thank You for creating all sorts of people.
Amen.

Not Guilty

. . . so that having been justified by His grace, we may become heirs with the hope of eternal life.

Titus 3:7 HCSB

The young man—husband, father, and small business owner—was on trial for a crime he didn't commit. There was much circumstantial evidence, however, so the outcome didn't seem promising. After days of hearing testimony, the man stood nervously waiting as the judge prepared to read the jury's decision . . .

Not guilty! The man's slate was wiped clean.

One day, each of us will stand before our Judge, God Himself. Even if you've accepted Jesus Christ as your Savior and Lord, you, too, will be judged. When you appear before God, however, you'll have the ultimate advantage: you'll be covered by the blood of Jesus. Consequently, when your divine Judge looks at you, He'll see not your sins, but the cleansing blood of His own Son. Then He'll declare you *not guilty!* And your slate will be wiped clean, as though you'd never even sinned in your life.

How amazing, Lord, that You would declare me "not guilty"—in spite of all I've done! Thank You for Your amazing love and grace. Amen.

Your Bethel

Jacob took the stone . . . and then poured oil on top of it to commemorate his experience with God. He named that place Bethel, which means "house of God."

Genesis 28:18–19 THE VOICE

As the silver-haired woman made her way across the open field, she realized she hadn't visited the place in thirty years . . . yet the feelings hadn't faded a bit. The farther she walked, the more her heart fluttered with anticipation. Finally, she crested a hill, and there it was: the old, gnarled tree; the pond; the boulder shaped like an elephant. This was the place her beloved husband had proposed some sixty years earlier.

Just as certain places become very special because they evoke beautiful memories, so an everyday place can become holy because God shows up there. That's what happened to Jacob at Bethel, and it can happen in your own home if you consistently invite God's presence to dwell there. God's love can transform your own humble living room, breakfast nook, or back porch into a place that is holy and His.

Where do you most often feel God's love? Where is your Bethel?

You're so welcome in my home, Lord. Please saturate every room with Your love so that my whole family feels Your presence. Amen.

Our Navigational Instrument

All Scripture is God-breathed and is useful for teaching, rebuking, correcting and training in righteousness.

2 Timothy 3:16

The sextant, a navigational instrument used primarily to determine the latitude and longitude of a ship, is believed to have been first described by Sir Isaac Newton in the 1600s. Sextants are still used today as backup to electronic equipment. But, because it's extremely sensitive, a sextant can be easily knocked out of adjustment, causing errors in the readings.

We have a navigational instrument, however, that's never inaccurate—the Bible. We can always depend upon its unchanging truths. The laws and advice given in God's Word are as true and accurate today as they were when it was written. Isn't it reassuring to know that what was true so many years ago is still just as true? God's love for us is poured out on every page of the Bible, from the creation described in Genesis to the last word of Revelation. It's His love letter—and navigational guide—to us!

Thank You, Lord, for Your true and never-changing Word. Help me remember to always turn to it to guide me through life. Amen.

God Relents

When God saw what they did, how they turned from their evil way,
God relented of the disaster that he had said he would do to them,
and he did not do it.

Jonah 3:10 ESV

The teenaged girl walked slowly down the stairs, reluctant to face her parents. Because her mother had to work late yesterday, she'd asked her daughter to take supper to the elderly lady next door. But the girl had forgotten. She felt certain she'd be grounded, and this evening was the school dance. And poor Mrs. Markham! Had she had any supper?

When the girl's parents heard what had happened, their first reaction was, indeed, to ground her; however, when they saw her tears of sorrow for Mrs. Markham, they relented. Surely her sorrow and concern for the woman was punishment enough.

In the story of Jonah, God sent the prophet to warn the people of Nineveh of His plans to destroy the city if they didn't repent for their sinful ways. When the people heard God's warning, they mourned for their sins. And God relented! In His great love, He gave them a second chance.

Thank You, Lord, that You are a just God, but also a loving God.
And thank You for all the second chances You give to me. Amen.

God's Conduits

*The LORD moved the heart of Cyrus king of Persia [to proclaim]: . . .
"The LORD . . . has appointed me to build a temple for him
at Jerusalem. . . . Any of his people among you may go up to
Jerusalem . . . and build the temple of the LORD."*

Ezra 1:1–3

When people want fresh water to be carried from one point to another without having to tote it in buckets or jugs, they must provide a conduit, or pipeline, of some sort to carry it for them. In ancient days, the Romans built huge, bridge-like structures, called *aqueducts*, to transport water. Today in the United States, huge pipes carry water to an area where it's treated, and then smaller pipes carry it out to cities, towns, homes, and businesses.

God also uses conduits to carry His Word. Amazingly, some of those conduits don't even worship Him. One such unbeliever was Cyrus, king of Persia. The Hebrew people were his captives when God determined He wanted His temple in Jerusalem rebuilt. Consequently, God used Cyrus as His unlikely conduit to send His people back to Jerusalem to rebuild the temple. Our God, in His love for us, will make sure His Word is carried where He wants it to go.

*Lord, You often use the most unlikely people to carry out Your plans.
So here I am, God; please use me. Amen.*

No Regrets

A broken spirit, O God, a heart that honestly regrets the past, You won't detest.

Psalm 51:17 THE VOICE

It's been said, "The worst thing to live with is regret." It must also be the most terrible thing to die with. Sadly, many people come to the end of their lives only to discover that they have some deep regrets: They didn't spend time with their kids. They cheated on a spouse. They never went to college.

But here's good news—although countless people have lamented the fact that they didn't spend their lives serving God, it's safe to say that no one, at the end of his or her life, has regretted having loved God. If you're a believer, you can take joy in the fact that your life is already a triumph simply because you belong to Him and love Him. Yes, you're sure to make more mistakes before you die, but you'll never regret the things you did for His kingdom, or the time you spent worshiping Him, or the simple fact that you love Him.

If there's one thing I know I'm doing that's worthwhile and priceless, it's loving You, Lord. Amen.

Love Is Patient

They who wait for the LORD shall renew their strength; they shall mount up with wings like eagles; they shall run and not be weary; they shall walk and not faint.

Isaiah 40:31 ESV

There's a humorous story about a husband who walks into the kitchen on a Sunday morning, expecting to see his breakfast on the table. But what he sees, instead, is his wife walking out the door. When he asks, "Where's our breakfast?" she replies, "We're trading roles today. You fix breakfast and get the kids ready for church. I'm going to sit outside in the car and honk the horn!" Mom's patience had obviously been exhausted.

When God seems to be taking an inordinately long time to answer your prayers, do you patiently wait for Him? Saint Augustine's mother prayed for her wayward son to get right with God for thirty years![4] Reread today's verse and think about the rewards of patiently waiting on God: strength, endurance, perseverance, courage, and answers to your prayers. Love is patient, so show your love for God by waiting patiently for His answers.

Lord, help me to be patient with my family and friends, with my boss and coworkers, and with You. After all, You are so very patient with me. Amen.

Love Leads

You yourself must be an example to them by doing good works of
every kind. Let everything you do reflect the integrity and seriousness
of your teaching.

Titus 2:7 NLT

- In 2014, the gap in pay between those without a degree and college graduates reached an all-time high.
- College students are in high demand in the workforce.
- The biggest economic advantage belongs to people who get a four-year degree.[5]

*I*f a father recited these statistics to his resistant teen, hoping she'd start applying to college, how likely is it he'd get the results he wanted? Not very. Love doesn't try to coerce with facts; instead, it leads with gentleness, and often by example. In this scenario, a father-daughter trip to a nearby college would be far more meaningful for the daughter. Or think of how compelling it would be if Dad took an evening class at the local college to improve his own career.

If you've been trying to talk someone into some course of action, remember that love doesn't force its way through; it leads.

Is there someone I've been trying to coerce into doing what I think is
right? Lead me, Lord, so I can lead with love. Amen.

Good and Trouble

Shall we accept good from God, and not trouble?

Job 2:10

A parent who sees his son heading down a destructive path doles out a stiff punishment.

A CEO denies her best employee a promotion because she knows an even better position is opening soon.

A coach knows her track team is ready to take the state championship, so she challenges them to the point of discomfort and sacrifice.

Every good leader—whether parent, teacher, coach, or boss—must sometimes say no, take away privileges, administer discipline, or in some way cause discomfort. In fact, it's sometimes the most promising student, son, daughter, or athlete who endures the most suffering because the person in charge sees the potential inside.

Because God is the perfect loving Parent, He, too, will sometimes give and sometimes take away. He says yes to some requests, but no to others. Trust Him. Even when you don't understand what He's up to, He *always* acts out of love . . . because He sees the potential inside.

I choose to accept all that You have for me, even the discipline, difficulties, and challenges. Because I know everything You do is out of love. Amen.

The List

For we are God's handiwork.

Ephesians 2:10

Have you ever seen a young woman write a wish list of attributes while dreaming of her future husband? She knows that much of her life will involve her future spouse, so she puts plenty of thought into it: *blue eyes . . . a wonderful sense of humor . . . a heart of integrity . . .* The details are very important because she'll one day give her heart to this person.

God has chosen to give His heart to us, His people—and that includes you. Imagine Him listing all the details as He dreamed you into being: *I want a freckle right there, and I think I'll make her tall and willowy—five feet ten inches—perfect! And I want him to love baseball and gardening . . .*

You aren't random. You're not an afterthought. You are a meticulously designed human being, priceless to—and profoundly loved by—your God.

Lord, You know and care about every little part of me—even the things I don't know about myself! Thank You for designing me as You did. Amen.

Equal Love

Yes, and I ask you . . . help these women since they have contended at my side in the cause of the gospel.

Equal rights for women has been a decades-long fight in America. In 1848, a group of women started a movement to gain equal rights, including the right to vote. Despite their efforts, and the efforts of many other women, it was 1920 before all women in the United States won the right to vote. Interestingly, it was in Wyoming, in 1869, that an all-male legislature first voted to give women in that territory the right to vote.

Almost two millennia earlier, the apostle Paul wrote to the new Christian church in Philippi, asking the church to "help these women since they have contended at my side." Paul knew that many women were instrumental in helping to spread the gospel of Christ. The Bible tells us that "there is neither Jew nor Gentile, neither slave nor free, nor is there male and female, for you are all one in Christ Jesus" (Galatians 3:28). God is not partial. He loves us all!

Thank You, Lord, for loving each one of us equally and for declaring each of us is equal before You. Amen.

Expectation

When they cry out to the LORD because of their oppressors, he will send them a savior and defender, and he will rescue them.

Isaiah 19:20

xpectation. What's more exciting than to eagerly await a person or an event? Perhaps it's Christmas, a new baby, loved ones we haven't seen for far too long, graduation, a fishing trip. Any of these can stir up excited feelings of anticipation.

So consider the almost frenzied expectation of the Hebrew people under by Roman rule. God had promised them a Messiah, a Savior, a Rescuer to save them from this relentless oppression. Little did they know that God would send them far more than they asked for.

Do you feel this kind of hopeful expectation when you ask the Lord to work in your life or in the lives of your friends or loved ones? Do you pray expecting Him to answer? Jesus said, "If you believe, you will receive whatever you ask for in prayer" (Matthew 21:22). Do you really believe what Jesus said? Believe expectantly! Your loving God just might grant you far more than you asked for.

Dear Lord, please teach me to pray with hope, expecting You to answer—and in ways I never even imagined! Amen.

Looking Back

I sought the Lord, and he answered me; he delivered me from all my fears.

Psalm 34:4

One of the most hair-raising scenes in the movie *Jurassic Park* involves a carload of people being chased by an enraged tyrannosaurus. As a terrified scientist looks into the rear view mirror, all he sees is a mouthful of fangs and this warning etched into the glass: OBJECTS IN MIRROR ARE CLOSER THAN THEY APPEAR.

That T. rex somehow became even more frightening while chasing the car than it had been when viewed head-on. But some things, like life's most difficult circumstances, are much *better* when we look back at them. When a difficult season is in the rearview mirror, so to speak, it's then that we have the perspective to see God's love for us in the midst of the pain, sorrow, or fear. We can finally see that even though we were hurting, uncomfortable, scared, or lonely, He was there, loving us relentlessly. Just as He always is.

Lord, when I look back at the difficult times in my life, I see how Your protection and love surrounded me. Thank You! Amen.

When There's No Room

Then [Mary] gave birth to her firstborn Son, and she wrapped Him
snugly in cloth and laid Him in a feeding trough—because there was
no room for them at the lodging place.

Luke 2:7 HCSB

"I can't possibly take on anything more; there's just no room in my day."

Sometimes it's good—and even wise—to say no to further demands on our time. But what if the thing we're saying no to is the most important thing we should be doing? If we truly want to do the wisest thing, shouldn't we be digging into the Bible daily?

We hear a lot today about prioritizing. When we prioritize, however, we should always keep the most important thing as *the most important thing*. And number one on our priority list should be time with the Lord. Even Jesus, when He was on earth, frequently went off to be alone with His Father—*our* Father. Imagine how He must feel when we tell Him there's no room in our lives for Him! If we truly love God, we'll ache to spend time with Him. Make room in your day for Him—every day.

Lord, I'm sorry for the times I've thought I didn't have enough time
for You. May You be my number one priority. Amen.

From Heaven to Manger

They hurried to the village and found Mary and Joseph. And there was the baby, lying in the manger.

Luke 2:16 NLT

He is a king. In fact, He's the King of kings. Yet, when He chose—willingly—to leave the glories of heaven to come to earth, He came not as a king, but as a baby. Not on a throne, but in the feeding trough of a stable. Not wrapped in exquisite robes, but swaddled in strips of cloth. Attending Him, besides His earthly mother and foster father, were cows, donkeys, and sheep. Jesus didn't come as royalty; He came as a servant.

And He came for one purpose: to save us.

In His thirty-three years on earth, Jesus felt all the pain, heartache, and suffering we experience. He felt the bitter cold and the relentless heat; the temptations, rejection, loss, and torture. Why did He leave heaven? Why did He suffer and die? His purpose was to take the shackles of our sins and set us free. His reason was love.

Lord, Your love for me is beyond measure. Thank You for choosing to come to earth so that I can one day live with You in heaven. Amen.

God's Plans

"For I know the plans I have for you," declares the LORD, "plans to prosper you and not to harm you, plans to give you hope and a future."

Jeremiah 29:11

Like most elderly people, the old woman loved to reminisce, especially about the happy times. This time, however, her thoughts were sober, her eyes shadowed. As she looked up at her young visitor, she shook her gray head. "No, when I look back on my life, I see that almost nothing worked out the way I had planned it. It seemed that every time I was ready to take a step, something stopped me, and I had to take a different path." Then the familiar twinkle returned to her eyes. "Thank God that He kept me from following *my* plans! *His* plans were so much better!"

God's plans are *always* better. He wants you to have "hope and a future." When it seems as if He's twisted your plans all out of shape, just wait patiently on Him. You'll find that, because of His great love for you, His plans will have the perfect shape!

Lord, rein me in when I insist on following my own way—I know Your plans for me are far better. Teach me to humbly submit to You. Amen.

To Love What Jesus Loves

Find out what pleases the Lord.

Ephesians 5:10

When we love someone, we naturally want to please that person. Therefore, it's important for us to know what he or she enjoys. For example, if a spouse, child, or friend is crazy about sci-fi, we might go out of our way to take him to see the newest movie. But it's also important to find out what *displeases* a loved one so we can avoid that as much as possible.

Shouldn't we do the same for the Lord? The coming new year is a perfect time to ask God if there's anything in your life that displeases Him—such as fear, bitterness, pride, or an unforgiving heart—and then allow Him to do away with it.

Does the thought of asking God to do an out-with-the-old, in-with-the-new overhaul in your life make you nervous? Just remember: when the Lord cleans house, you become more like Him, paving the way for a new year filled with joy, contentment, and fruitfulness.

Lord, I invite You to "clean house" during this coming New Year's season. Make me more like You. Amen.

The Greatest Love of All

This is how God showed his love among us: He sent his one and only
Son into the world that we might live through him.

1 John 4:9

In 1985, Whitney Houston released her song "Greatest Love of All." It had already been recorded by George Benson in 1977 and did well on the R&B charts, but few would argue that Whitney's rendition is the one we all remember. Its lyrics include sentiments like, "I learned to depend on me" and, "Learning to love yourself is the greatest love of all." The song resonated with many people in a world where self-adulation is the goal.

Contrary to this much-recorded song, the greatest love of all is God Himself. And He doesn't just love; He *is* love. The greatest love we can ever experience. And the greatest act of love a person can achieve is to love God. In fact, if we love Him as we should—with all our hearts, souls, minds, and strength—we won't have time for vanity and pride. We'll be so busy looking at Him that we won't even notice ourselves.

The greatest love I'll ever know is You, dear God. Help me to love
You with all that I am—heart, soul, mind, and strength. Amen.

Forgiveness: We All Need It

"If you forgive other people when they sin against you, your heavenly Father will also forgive you. But if you do not forgive others their sins, your Father will not forgive your sins."

Matthew 6:14–15

Your neighbor invites your son to join his son's baseball team, but you gently turn the offer down, saying your son is too young to play team sports. Your neighbor laughs and says you're an overprotective parent. You storm home, determined you'll never forgive him.

When Jesus' apostles asked Him to teach them how to pray, Jesus taught them what we today call "the Lord's Prayer"—words many Christians know by heart. However, immediately after that, He taught them about forgiveness in Matthew 6:14–15, two verses we often seem to ignore.

Yes, God loves you. Yes, His love is unconditional. But . . . He loves your neighbor just as much as He loves you! And He knows that the neighbor who has offended you needs your forgiveness every bit as much as you do.

Let's stop expecting God to forgive us when we don't forgive others. Forgive the one who's offended you—today.

Heavenly Father, please forgive me for not having forgiven others. Soften my heart so that I can forgive those who have offended me. Amen.

The Need for Hope

Praise be to the God and Father of our Lord Jesus Christ! In his great mercy he has given us new birth into a living hope.

1 Peter 1:3

Sometimes the best part of a vacation is planning for it. We don't even think about the possibility of bad weather; we're confident the weather's going to be ideal all week, the activities are going to be safe and fun, the car's going to function perfectly, the scenery will be superb. Without this hopeful attitude, planning the trip would be scary and threatening and no fun at all. We all need hope.

In many of the Old Testament books, God's prophets warned the Hebrew people that they would face calamities if they didn't straighten up and fly right. Again and again the people drifted away from the Lord and His teachings. Again and again, God sent prophets to warn them. But God knew even people who need to be rebuked also need hope. Therefore, He frequently added a promise to His warnings: He *did* love His people; He *would* deliver them; His kingdom *would* be established on earth.

Even when I fail You, Lord, You're there to pick me up, remind me that You love me, and encourage me to try again. Thank You. Amen.

Love That Transforms

"As the Father has loved me, so have I loved you."

John 15:9

ove. What other word evokes such a range of emotions? Joy, pride, envy, bitterness, rejection, thrill, lust, anger, excitement . . . and more. There are those who would give their lives for it, others who would literally kill for it. Libraries overflow with books about it, movies tempt and terrify with it. And yet love, in its truest form, is intended to bring only good and favorable responses. In fact, love's purpose is to transform the world.

That's what Jesus' love for us does; it transforms us from sinners into saints. Because Jesus loves us so completely and purely, He gave His very life for us. And, almost two thousand years later, He continues to rejoice in every person who comes to Him and to grieve over every person who denies He is Lord. Nothing can turn His love from you. Won't you give Him the greatest gift you can—your heart—today?

Lord, I give You my heart, my life, my all. You are my Lord! Amen.

Notes

January

1. Ian Austen, "The Comma That Costs 1 Million Dollars (Canadian)," *New York Times*, October 25, 2016, http://www.nytimes.com /2006/10/25/business/worldbusiness/25comma.html.
2. *Brennan*, dir. by David Leo Schultz (2016; Color Green Films).

February

1. Jill Reilly, "Couple Who Never Spent a Day Apart in 68 Years of Marriage Die Within Hours of Each Other," DailyMail.com, June 26, 2014, http://www.dailymail.co.uk/news/article-2670490 /Couple-never-spent-day-apart-68-years-marriage-die-just-10 -hours-apart.html.
2. David Roberts, "Everest 1953: First Footsteps—Sir Edmund Hillary and Tenzing Norgay," NationalGeographic.com, March 3, 2013, https://www.nationalgeographic.com/adventure/features/everest /sir-edmund-hillary-tenzing-norgay-1953/.
3. Joel Landau, "'Mysterious Voice' Leads Police to Baby in Submerged Car," *New York Daily News*, March 10, 2015, http://www.nydailynews .com/news/national/mysterious-voice-leads-police-baby-car-crash -article-1.2142732.

March

1. Sarah Whitman-Salkin, "In Search of the $10,000 Spice," Daily Beast, July 14, 2009, https://www.thedailybeast.com/in-search -of-the-dollar10000-spice.
2. "Marriage and Divorce," American Psychological Association, accessed February 5, 2018, http://www.apa.org/topics/divorce/.

April

1. "Founder and Pastor, Bill Wilson," Metro World Child, accessed February 6, 2018, http://www.metroworldchild.org/about-us /bill-wilson.

2. Carey Lodge, "First Christian Convert in Tribe That Killed Jim Elliot and Four Other Missionaries Dies," *Christian Today*, April 15, 2014, https://www.christiantoday.com/article/first-christian -believer-of-the-tribe-that-killed-jim-elliot-and-four-other -missionaries-dies/36817.htm.

3. Henri J. M. Nouwen, *Life of the Beloved* (New York: Crossroad Publishing Company, 2002).

4. Jerry Bridges, *The Gospel for Real Life: Turn to the Liberating Power of the Cross . . . Every Day* (Carol Stream, IL: NavPress, 2003).

5. Alison Schwartz, "Inside the Image: Hero Carlos Arredondo Helps Boston Marathon Bombing Victim," People.com, April 16, 2013, http://people.com/human-interest/carlos-arredondo-hero-in -boston-marathon-bombing/.

6. Matt Woodley, "Catalyst 2011 Andy Stanley: Be Present," *Christianity Today*, accessed February 9, 2018, http://www.christianitytoday .com/pastors/2011/october-online-only/catalyst-2011-andy -stanley-be-present.html.

May

1. Shannon L. Alder quotes, Goodreads, accessed February 16, 2018, https://www.goodreads.com/quotes/911205-when-dealing-with -critics-always-remember-this-critics-judge-things.

2. Gary Chapman, *The 5 Love Languages* (Chicago: Northfield, 1992).

3. Associated Press, "RadioShack Layoff Notices Are Sent by E-Mail," *New York Times*, August 31, 2006, http://www.nytimes.com /2006/08/31/business/31radio.html.

4. "Insomnia," Sleep Health Foundation, accessed February 9, 2018, http://sleephealthfoundation.org.au/pdfs/Insomnia.pdf.

June

1. Anita Sanchez, "Ten Things You Might Not Know About Dandelions," Maine Organic Farmers and Gardeners Association,

accessed February 9, 2018, http://www.mofga.org/Default
.aspx?tabid=756.

2. "Step-mom Adult Adoption Surprise!" posted by AutumnRoseVlogs,
May 14, 2017, YouTube video, https://www.youtube.com/watch
?v=cUIRyI1kIrE.

3. Sarah Young, *Jesus Calling*, (Nashville, Thomas Nelson, 2004), 139.

4. *Merriam-Webster*, s.v. "success," accessed February 6, 2018.
https://www.merriam-webster.com/dictionary/success.

5. "Your Presence Is Fullness of Joy," *Sermon Central*, accessed February
16, 2018, https://www.sermoncentral.com/sermons/your-presence
-is-fullness-of-joy-sol-madlambayan-sermon-on-joy-62405.

6. *Merriam-Webster*, s.v. "holy," accessed February 6, 2018.
https://www.merriam-webster.com/dictionary/holy.

7. Mayo Clinic Staff, "Chronic Stress Puts Your Health at Risk," Mayo
Clinic, April 21, 2016, http://www.mayoclinic.org/healthy-lifestyle
/stress-management/in-depth/stress/art-20046037.

July

1. "Clemency Statistics," United States Department of Justice, accessed
February 7, 2018, https://www.justice.gov/pardon/clemency
-statistics.

2. "The Man Who Refused a Pardon," CBMC International, accessed
February 7, 2018, http://www.cbmcint.com/the-man-who-refused
-a-pardon/.

August

1. "La Maison Picassiette," *Raw Vision*, accessed February 8, 2018,
https://rawvision.com/articles/la-maison-picassiette.

2. "Candy Lightner Biography," Biography.com, A&E Television
Networks, last updated May 23, 2016, https://www.biography.com
/people/candy-lightner-21173669.

3. "About Laura," LauraDekker.com, accessed February 8, 2018,
http://www.lauradekker.nl/English/Home.html.

4. Christopher Klein, "The Great Smog of 1952," December 6, 2012,
History.com, accessed February 16, 2018, http://www.history.com
/news/the-killer-fog-that-blanketed-london-60-years-ago.

5. *Merriam-Webster*, s.v. "mood," accessed February 8, 2018, https://www.merriam-webster.com/dictionary/mood.

6. "What Is SubTropolis?" Hunt Midwest, accessed February 8, 2018, https://huntmidwest.com/industrial-space-for-lease/what-is -subtropolis/.

September

1. "The Longest Migration—Yukon River King Salmon," Salmon World, August 17, 2016, accessed February 8, 2018, https://medium .com/@aksalmonworld/the-longest-migration-yukon-river-king -salmon-f0357e55ed44#.bnwubah3y.

2. E. Paul Baca, "Surreal Video of Postal Deliveries in Santa Rosa Neighborhood Destroyed by Fire," the *Mercury News*, October 11, 2017, https://www.mercurynews.com/2017/10/11/mail-carrier -delivers-to-devastated-santa-rosa-coffey-park/.

3. "Millennials Check Their Phones More Than 157 Times Per Day," *Social Media Week*, New York, May 31, 2016, https://socialmediaweek .org/newyork/2016/05/31/millennials-check-phones-157-times -per-day/.

4. Anna LeMind, "Interesting Facts About Human Memory," Learning-Mind.com, accessed February 8, 2018, https://www .learning-mind.com/interesting-facts-about-human-memory/.

5. Associated Press, "Geologists Study Massive Land O'Lakes Sinkhole," *Ledger*, last updated August 14, 2017, http://www.theledger.com /news/20170812/geologists-study-massive-land-olakes-sinkhole.

October

1. Colby Itkowitz, "Her Son Shot Their Daughters 10 Years Ago. Then, These Amish Families Embraced Her as a Friend," *Washington Post*, October 1, 2016, https://www.washingtonpost.com/news /inspired-life/wp/2016/10/01/10-years-ago-her-son-killed-amish -children-their-families-immediately-accepted-her-into-their -lives/?utm_term=.e6ec9796b043.

2. A. N. Wilson, *C. S. Lewis: A Biography*, (New York: W. W. Norton, 1990), 127.

3. Elie Wiesel, *US News & World Report*, October 27, 1986.

4. "Diamond Grading Guide: The 4 Cs Explained," *Hubspot*, accessed February 16, 2018, https://cdn2.hubspot.net/hubfs/300100/DAR _Diamond101Insert_Final.pdf?t=1489435025826 .

5. Robert W. Wood, "IRS Paid $5.8 Billion in Fraudulent Refunds, Identity Theft Efforts Need Work," *Forbes*, February 19, 2015, https://www.forbes.com/sites/robertwood/2015/02/19/irs-paid-5–8 -billion-in-fraudulent-refunds-identity-theft-efforts-need-work /#9a3c74a251f4.

6. Joseph Stromberg, "Experiments Show We Really Can Learn While We Sleep," Smithsonian.com, June 26, 2012, http://www .smithsonianmag.com/science-nature/experiments-show-we -really-can-learn-while-we-sleep-141518869/.

November

1. "Francis Chan: 7 Questions to Ask Before You Preach," October 20, 2014, *Sermon Central*, accessed February 16, 2018, https://www .sermoncentral.com/pastors-preaching-articles/francis-chan -francis-chan-7-questions-to-ask-before-you-preach-2037.

2. Cathal Dennehy, "Dennis Kimetto Breaks World Record at Berlin Marathon," *Runners World*, September 28, 2014, https://www. runnersworld.com/newswire/dennis-kimetto-breaks-world- record-at-berlin-marathon.

3. John Francis Xavier O'Conor, *A Study of Francis Thompson's Hound of Heaven* (n.p.: John Lane, 1912), 7.

4. Eric Liddell, *The Disciplines of the Christian Life* (Peabody, MA: eChristian Books, 2012).

5. Billy Graham, "Billy Graham: Bible Is God's 'Love Letter' to Us," *Seattle Post-Intelligencer*, September 6, 2007, https://www.seattlepi .com/news/article/Billy-Graham-Bible-is-God-s-love-letter -to-us-1246557.php.

6. TheFreeDictionary, s.v. "air cover," accessed February 9, 2018, https://www.thefreedictionary.com/air+cover.

7. Anne Lamott, *Bird by Bird: Some Instructions on Writing and Life* (New York: Knopf Doubleday, 2007), 22.

December

1. Brother Lawrence, *Practice of the Presence of God: The Best Rule of Holy Life*, "Fourth Conversation," Christian Classics Ethereal Library, accessed April 24, 2018, https://www.ccel.org/ccel/lawrence/practice.iii.iv.html

2. Unnamed minister, "One Thing," on Kevin Prosch's album *Palanquin* (Forerunner Records, 2002).

3. Associated Press, "60-Mile Traffic Jam in China May Last Weeks," *Fox News World*, August 24, 2010, http://www.foxnews.com/world/2010/08/24/long-haul-chinas-traffic-jam-stretching-long-km-weeks.html.

4. Cyril Orji, *An Introduction to Religious and Theological Studies* (Eugene, OR: Wipf and Stock, 2015), 131.

5. David Leonhardt, "Is College Worth It? Clearly, New Data Say," *The New York Times*, Mary 27, 2014, https://www.nytimes.com/2014/05/27/upshot/is-college-worth-it-clearly-new-data-say.html?_r=0.

Notes

Notes

Notes

Notes

Notes

Notes